Insights Into Martial Arts

Tai Ch'i, T.M. & Yoga

Selwyn R. Stevens, Ph.D.

Published by

Jubilee Resources International Inc.
Equipping Christians, Liberating Captives

Additional copies of this book are available from:

Jubilee Resources International Inc.

PO Box 3, Feilding 4740, New Zealand

or our secure Internet Webshop at

www.jubileeresources.org

ISBN 978-1-877203-12-1

Unless otherwise indicated, all Scripture quotations are taken from

The Holy Bible, New King James Version.

Your guarantee of accurate Information: various sources and authorities have been quoted in good faith throughout this book. Every attempt has been made to ensure these quotations are accurate and in context.

The author uses American English spelling, not the Queen's English.

I wish to say thank you to my good friend, brother in the Lord and armor-bearer, Andrew McIntosh, for his support and for granting permission to quote significantly from his research article on Tai Ch'i; and also to my friend Paul Simpson, for the basic outline of the prayer of Repentance on page 57.

Contents

Introduction

Millions around the world are involved in various Martial arts. Most get involved to improve health, fitness, confidence and their ability to protect themselves. Practitioners often claim that they are also taught principles of respect, courtesy and self-discipline. Martial Artist, Fay Goodman wrote, "The martial arts encourage us to fight the enemy within, in an effort to become better people." [1]

It is nice that Martial Artists are taught good things like respect and self discipline. What this author is describing is also a method of salvation without a savior. Only God can make people truly better.

There are many influences in our Western society, and not all of them are good for us. Some influences appear to be beneficial, but in fact are the proverbial "wolf in sheep's clothing." In other words, the apparent goodness of some thing or practice may in fact be harmful to us, even if this isn't obvious to us at the time.

We have many people who come to our ministry centre for help with various problems. Also, I have ministered personally with many people in my own country of New Zealand, and also in other countries. It never ceases to amaze me how gullible people get involved in things which are detrimental to their spiritual, as well as their physical and emotional health. The items covered in the title of this book are amongst those.

It is clear from my research these practices have negative spiritual, emotional and physical implications. Ignorance isn't bliss when there is a high price to pay for involvement in some things such as these.

Sometimes treated in the West as a health and exercise regime, Martial Arts are clearly much more, when we allow ourselves to investigate it fully. We need to check its roots, its origins. We need to check the fruit from it too - the consequences in people's lives.

This small book is intended to cover a vital need for basic information on these issues. It should provide an antidote, through repentance, prayer and ministry, for an effective liberation from the effects of Martial Arts, Tai Ch'i, TM and Yoga. Millions around the world need such liberation.

Origins & History:

Buddhist monks are thought to have taken Indian fighting techniques to China between the 5th and 6th centuries B.C. The most famous of the monks is claimed to be Bodihdharma, who in the late 5th century BC travelled to China from India and became the chief instructor of martial arts at the now-famous Shaolin monastery. As well as teaching yoga, Bodihdharma also taught the empty-hand fighting system known as Shaolin Kung Fu. Most of the Chinese martial arts are based on this early form.

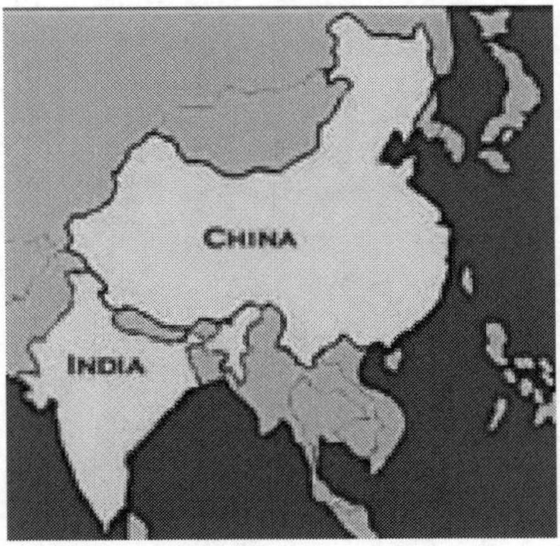

In both ancient India and ancient China, superstition, divination and spiritism were all in common use. In China, there was a belief that dragons slept on the corners of roofs, so the roofs were designed with upturned corners so the dragons wouldn't fall off. Andrew McIntosh records, "There were also specialists who advised the bereaved on how to place a dead body in such a way so as not to hinder the spirits leaving the grave."[2]

These and many other practices and beliefs gave philosophers ideas to explain the world and its workings. Immortality was sought, as well as greater understanding of the spiritual and natural worlds, and how these might relate to each other. The concept of Ch'i, and Yin and Yang were developed from this search for understanding.

Bob Larson wrote, *"The general history of the Martial Arts goes back to the dawn of civilisation in India and nearly three millennia in China, where it developed more extensively. By the establishment of the Feudal States in 770 BC, Kung Fu was widely practiced. Only during the Boxer Rebellion of 1900 were Martial Arts totally eliminated from the mainland. In 1928, they were renamed War Arts and were nationally re-accepted.*

Lao Tzu

Over the centuries various forms of the arts were modified and evolved into more or less violent intent. Northern and Southern, and hard and soft schools developed. Kung Fu was the original all-inclusive term describing the Martial Arts... Though one often thinks of the arts as "Made in Japan," they have many roots and cultural variations. But the religious foundation has common pagan origins.

The original religious philosophy of Kung Fu dates back as far as 2696 BC where it was rooted in the occultic forms of divination known as the I-Ching and the "Book of Changes." Lao Tzu, the Chinese-born sage born in 604BC, added further demonic embellishments. His teachings were set forth in a 5,280 word manuscript called "Tao te ching," often called the Tao or "the Way." He taught that salvation could not be found in prayer but rather by the observation of nature, the natural way. As the trees bend with the wind and the rivers follow the path of least resistance, so must man adapt this rhythm of coexistence with evil and wrong.

With the adoption of Taoism, Kung Fu developed into a complex system of occult practices that included contemplation and breathing exercises."[3]

"In the sixth century AD Bodihdharma (called Ta Mo in China) came to the Shaolin Monastery and seeing that the monks there were in poor physical condition from too much meditation and not enough movement, developed his Eighteen Form Lohan Exercise. Over time these grew to be the precursors of the Wei Chia (outer-extrinsic) school of exercise, by which is meant all the schools of kung fu and other martial art forms, which take an 'external' approach. This is in contrast to the Nei Chia (internal-intrinsic) school of which Tai Ch'i is a member, that take a fundamentally 'internal' approach. I believe that it is just as deadly as the other Martial Arts. The slow seemingly effortless movements when sped up and used on an opponent can be just as lethal."[4]

Shaolin

Shaolin means "small forest." During the reign of the Ching Dynasty (between 1662 and 1722), under the rule of Emperor K'anghsi, the Shaolin monastery Siu Lam, in the Honan province, became very powerful through its training in Kung Fu. Shaolin became such a threat to the Manchurian government, they sent troops to destroy it fearing an uprising. Some traitorous monks set fire to the monastery, and only a few of the monks escaped. They took their knowledge and practices with them.

What are the issues to consider?

As a Christian, there are two main questions which need to be answered about involvement in any of the items covered in this book. The first question is, *"Does the Lord Jesus want you involved in them?"*

The second question is *"If the Lord says He doesn't want us involved, is this something we should warn other Christians about?"*

There are some sincere Christians who feel justified in staying involved with their Martial Arts, or other practices. It isn't for me to question their commitment to Jesus Christ. Each of us will have to answer directly to Him in due time. Having said that, there are many who have been involved in various Martial Arts, Tai Ch'i, TM and Yoga, for example, and when they have seriously sought the Lord's opinion, He has convicted them to leave, and quite an number have been called to speak out or write against such involvements.

There are five main area Christians involved in these matters need to face when they seek God's views about these issues. I believe with honest soul-searching and heart examination, God will show people what He really wants for each of our lives. It is for the best.

Let us now look at these one by one.

1. Pride

Many who have been involved in these practices have developed, over time, an air of superiority over others. There can often be a self-sufficiency, due to the power and control taught and learned through these practices. Egotism and arrogance are very common problems with Martial Artists - probably more than many other people, with the possible exception of politicians. Many practitioners also idolize their Masters and Senseis, which is dangerously close to idolatry, for which God imposes judgement.

2. Violence

I have raised this issue with various Christian leaders who have ministered to people with a family history of Martial Arts involvement. All have said there has been evidence of violence in relationships, as well as passed down through family lines. Many Martial Arts techniques are seldom solely self-defensive, while most are offensive, aggressive and intended to cripple, maim or kill people. The tactics are retaliatory and intended to inflict punishment. Jesus Christ gave an example of love. Should the violent disposition in so many who practice Martial Arts, be found in Jesus' disciples?

3. Whose body is it?

For a Christian, the answer is that we are bought with the price of Calvary by Jesus Christ - we belong to Him, and we are to be the Temple of the Holy Spirit, allowing Him to work through us for the sake of His kingdom. Many of the blocks, kicks and punches from Martial Arts can be destructive and can also cause degeneration to many functions of our bodies. The rigorous training, sparring, breaking wooden timber and concrete blocks can, over time, bring arthritis, joint injuries and other health problems. Let's not forget the numerous bruising and even broken bones in the bodies of many Martial Artists. I question whether this is an appropriate use of our bodies we Christians know belong to God.

4. Occult Connection

There is no question about the occultic and Eastern mystical basis to most Martial Arts and the other issues being investigated in this book. Many commence training for self-defence, or physical exercise and discipline reasons, including sports competitions and other claimed health benefits However, a significant number are drawn into the occultic philosophies behind these arts. In my research, I have yet to find a single Martial Art system which could sit comfortably with a Christian/Biblical world-view. Since the God of the Bible pronounces very stern judgements on those involved in the occult, (see Deut. 18:9-

12; Galatians 5:20 -21), it doesn't seem to be enlightened self-interest to participate in it. We each have to answer to Him one day.

5. What is the Testimony to others?

A genuine Christian would want a testimony which doesn't become a stumbling block to others. Just as there can't be a "Christian" paedophile, or a "Christian" adulterer, or a "Christian" murderer, I haven't found any evidence to support a "Christian" Martial Artist, Tai Ch'i, TM or Yoga practitioner. The fundamental basis and philosophy behind all these is occultic. It is based in violence and has a spiritual power which at best is soulish, and at worst, probably demonic. I question what a genuine Christian would be doing in such a place. It is interesting that several of the former Martial Artists who tried to use their practice as a testimony for Jesus Christ, observed that far more of those they attracted got drawn to the philosophy and occult rather than to Jesus Christ. That's not good fruit. Bill Rudge, the Founder of the "Christian Martial Arts Association" states, *"Even before I was a Christian, a lot of my Karate associates who started training when I did at least professed to be Christians. But few, if any, were really committed. It is interesting to note that a few years later almost everyone who had continued in the martial arts now practiced yoga, meditation, or TM and some even considered themselves Zen Buddhists or Taoists."*[5]

Some belong to groups with names like "Karate for Christ" or "Judo for Jesus." The problem is that in their demonstrations in schools and churches, they have witnessed at least as much for the practice as they have for Christ. That seems like a mixed message at best. The problem seems to be not whether they are offending their own conscience, but whether they are misleading others who are ignorant of the accompanying spiritual and other related issues. As former Spiritualist medium, Ben Alexander states, *"Remember, it is not karate that wins people to Christ. It can possibly have the opposite effect."* [6]

Most Martial Arts and related fields have a senior figure called a "Master." This title may also be found in other occultic practices or organisations including Freemasonry, other secret societies and lodges, and Reiki. However, Jesus commanded that we are to call no man "master" in Matthew 23:10.

Is It "Just Exercise?"

"Martial" means "Of or appropriate to warfare," or warlike, from the Latin, "Martialis," meaning that belonging to Mars, the god of war; according to the Oxford Dictionary.

The teaching and foundational philosophy behind all Martial Arts is directly opposed to the teachings of Jesus Christ. He told His followers to "Turn the other check;" and also to "forgive them for they know not what they do." While Jesus could have resisted his torturers and false accusers, He fulfilled Isaiah 53:7 "he opened not his mouth." According to Peter - who saw most of what was inflicted on Jesus, stated "...when he suffered, he threatened not, but committed himself to Him that judges righteously," (1 Peter 2:23). Jesus wasn't a wimp - He had total confidence that His life and purposes were in His Father's hands. It is called "trust."

Many who are or were involved in Martial Arts were seeking "self-defence skills" because of the possibility of violence they may encounter. In several cases the violence had already occurred when they were younger. Sometimes that violence was physical, other times verbal, but the effects were often just as damaging. Some were bullied at school; others had an abusive parent or spouse. There is some research suggesting those who came from an abusive home often marry into another abusive home. I would like to see some serious academic-level research into the generational iniquity issues of such a problem, as anecdotally there seems to be a connection.

Some of the people who learn Martial Arts - without them being consciously aware of this - will project a spirit of violence onto their spouse, family and even workmates. These people near them often sense in their spirits that there is a form of danger in the martial artist. So they often tend to walk on eggshells around them to avoid triggering a violent reaction. This shows me that there is a spiritual dimension to Martial Arts which many haven't noticed, nevertheless they can see the effects, or fruit.

Most people involved in these practices have been told they are just harmless exercise to develop physical health improvements, sometimes with additional benefits to one's emotional or mental health. Seldom are they told up front that there is a spiritual dimension to all these practices, although this is frequently mentioned in writings about them. Maybe it is the quick-fix society which is too busy to do proper research about the subject.

In my experience, and that of many pastors and counselors I have spoken with, there is a supernatural element or dimension to these topics which is highly suspect at even a cursory glance.

Bob Larson wrote, *"Whether the form of martial art one practices is based on the doctrine of naturalism found in Taoism, or the doctrine of illusion found in Buddhism, the philosophical basis of both explicitly deny the blood atonement of Christ. The Christian practitioner of the martial arts must ask himself whether or not any involvement in such physical disciplines implies an inherent approval of the religious principles behind them."* [7] In a later revision he adds, *"He should also take care to be certain his instructor adequately divorces the mystical aspects of the martial arts from their strictly physical components."* [7]

New Zealand Evangelist, Rev. Barry Smith, in his book 'Second Warning' writes of martial arts:

(a) *"Martial arts are demonic*

(b) As you bow to the master, or a picture of him, you bow to a spirit of violence who is in that man

(c) As you do your deep breathing exercises, you breathe in an Eastern spirit of violence. Your breath is actually reserved for the Spirit of God.

(d) The continual longing for someone to attack you, comes from this proud spirit of violence that inhabits you, upon your clear invitation."[8]

While these writers may use different words, there is a consistent warning about the nature and consequences of martial arts.

Energy - The Psychic Component

Supernatural energy can only come from one of two sources - God, or Satan. God often gives people His power and it is seen in the miracles recorded in the Bible and often seen today. The energy here comes from God. It isn't latent in the person God is using. There is no reputable scientific proof that humans have latent, natural, neutral energies available to be developed. If they do have "energy" it isn't electromagnetic, gravitational or nuclear and which is scientifically undetectable. Apart from God any "energy" which is supernatural or spiritual must come from Satan. All the evidence to date shows this energy is sourced in the occult realm, and is psychic or demonic.

Human users may falsely believe they have special powers within themselves. Shamans, witchdoctors, Hindu holy men and many others willingly admit they have no powers themselves, but acknowledge their power or energy comes exclusively from the spirits. God forbids human involvement in the occult/spirit realm. Any such contact is with forces and beings alien and hostile to Him. Those involved come into contact with demonic spirits. If you are involved in any practices which include psychic energy you have now been warned about their true nature and the consequences.

The two best known psychic energies are Prana and Ch'i.

Prana

Prana is the Hindu/Yogic energy involving the potentially lethal rising of the serpent Kundalini. It is claimed to reside at the base of the spine and is aroused through Yoga. As it rises towards the Middle Eye on the forehead it opens Chakras and gives psychic powers. These are claimed to enable the user to control their mind and body and even the whole universe, thus they become god or part of god.

According to Vivekananda "mind healers, faith healers, Spiritualists, Christian Scientists, hypnotists and so on... (have) at the back of each the control of Prana, whether they know it or not." Wilson and Weldon say "Prana is truly a demonic energy output in seances, witchcraft, psychokinesis, psi-healing, etc."[9]

Kundalini

According to the Hindus, a dangerous snake is lurking in every human being. Her name is Kundalini and she lies curled up at the base of the spine. Remember that one of the devil's biblical names is "serpent." In Taoism the tan tien, claimed to be the psychic centre of the soul is located in the same region, [7] cm. below the navel. It is recommended not to wake the serpent without the help of a Guru. Gurus teach that if the serpent raises her head and is released without control, she raves, and no man can resist her power. In Hinduism a guru is a "God" who seeks to help people achieve "God" status so that they can break free from the reincarnation curse and reach the state of absolute nothingness known as Nirvana. One has to wonder though, for if a guru is really a "God" they should already be in Nirvana, not on earth. This indicates that they can't have actually reached ultimate enlightenment themselves!

The name Guru translates sin (Gu) destroyer (Ru), which is a title that only Jesus Christ is deserving of. If you take the letters Kali out of Kundalini you get the name of the Hindu serpent goddess of death, destruction and peace. She is depicted with serpents coming out of her head, much like the Gorgon Medusa from Greek Mythology. People who are demonized by Kali often experience lower back pain, joint pains, headaches, and depression, until the demon is cast out of them in Jesus Name! For the Hindus, the snake Kundalini symbolizes the hidden supernatural energy slumbering in every man. A special form of Yoga is designed to release her power, called Kundalini Yoga (Tai Ch'i is also known as Chinese Yoga). Interestingly Tai Ch'i traces its roots back to approximately the 2nd millennium B.C. to the practice of yoga in ancient India.

In China, yoga came to be developed into what is called Saolin chuan ("chuan," means boxing). In the 13th century AD, a Taoist monk by the name of Chang Sang Feng reputedly developed what has come to be known as Tai Ch'i. Yoga in the original Sanskrit translates, "to yoke oneself with Brahmin," who of course is yet another false god. Yoga is a form of Hinduism, and also has the ultimate goal for the practitioner of achieving "God" status. When the snake is awakened, she is believed to move along fine channels, known as the Chakras, until she reaches the heart, where she takes up her new home. The significance of this is that some psychics say that there is a connection between Kundalini energy and the Chinese energy known as "Ch'i." The channels followed by the snake correspond to the acupuncture channels, which are known as meridians. Acupuncture, psychics say, is no different from a controlled manipulation of the snake Kundalini, as practiced in Kundalini Yoga. This has lead Dr. Hiroshi Motoyama, director of the Institute for Religious Psychology in Tokyo to claim *"The acupuncture points are the points where Western Medicine, the Chinese medicine and Indian Yoga meet."*[10]

Ch'i

The Taoists of ancient China believed in the existence of an energy they called "Ch'i." They claimed it flowed through all the universe (including human bodies and organs) along invisible energy lines called meridians. The Yin and the Yang are the two opposing yet harmonizing forces which are claimed to control this energy. They do not cancel each other out nor are they antagonistic. They are parts of the whole. Both Prana and Ch'i are claimed to be the "essential vital force" of all creation. In other words the universe is god, and since we humans are part of the universe it follows we must be part of god. This spiritual concept was powerfully promoted through the cult movie series, "Star Wars" - the "Let the Force (false impersonal god) be with you." Many Christians, despite enjoying the general entertainment of the movies also didn't agree with the spiritual message it was conveying to a largely untaught and spiritually naive Western culture. These concepts cannot be separated from their occultic roots. The overwhelming evidence is that psychic energy requires a spirit or demon to operate it.

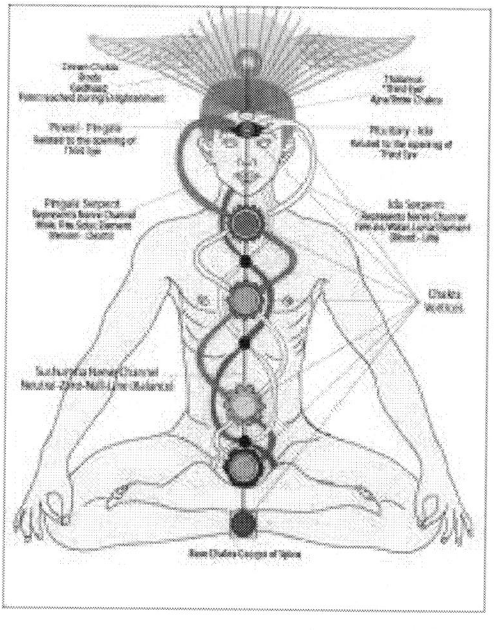

The concepts of Yin and Yang are both philosophical and religious. It teaches that all things emanate, or flow from the Tao, and there are elements of this 'flow' which are contrary to each other. For one to achieve the ultimate is to have all things flowing in harmony.

The symbol of Yin and Yang have also been called the "Chinese good luck" sign. These believers claim that if an imbalance between Yin and Yang should occur, then illness results. Acupuncture, Reflexology, Shiatsu and a number of other related zone therapies were developed to treat this claimed imbalance and to help restore harmony and healing. This is psychic healing, or in other words they use supernatural energy empowered by evil spirits.

Ch'i imbalances or disturbances are believed by Taoist practitioners to be caused by an unbalanced diet, emotional disturbances, and climatic conditions during hot or cold weather. They will often prescribe a diet and suggest exercise programme postures to sit or stand, and even the way you should sleep, to influence the flow of Ch'i.

Yin	*Yang*
dark	light
yielding	firm
moon	sun
west/north	east/south
night	day
metal	wood
cold	heat
white/black	green/red
water	fire
rest	movement
dampness	dryness
autumn/winter	spring/summer
interior	exterior
female	male
below	above
contraction	expansion
negative	positive
death	life
inaction	action
evil	good

According to the Taoists and New Age occultists, they can manipulate your body to release the "blockage of energy" in your system and then you can become well. Most Alternative Therapists do body manipulation, massages and even diagnostic procedures, so that by the time you come out of the clinic you feel different. Something has happened to you. What they call "Energy" has been put into you. But the energy they are describing is not a natural or scientific energy. The energy they put into you is a demon. They channel a spirit into your body. I believe that is why they want to put their hands on you. It makes you feel different, because when a spirit is channeled into a human body, it causes a number of changes, including psychological and physiological, and these can even change your blood pressure so you feel different.

The Taoist therefore is led to believe that he can lead a fulfilling and harmonious life by his blending in with the 'cycles of the universe' and by achieving a 'proper interaction of these forces.'

The Chinese saw that in the cycles of nature there was a rhythm, e.g. summer-winter, light-darkness, warm-cold, etc. They thus reasoned that rain and sunshine (Yang) fall on the earth (Yin) and the crops grow.

Thus the passive is said to yield to the aggressive, but by yielding, the passive is said to absorb and overcome. It is this very same principle that Gandhi, the famous Indian Guru, employed in his fight to expel the British from India. He succeeded and achieved India's independence from the colonial British Empire.

Again, it is this same concept that one finds in martial arts. The student is taught that the Shaolin monk walked the 'right path' while those in opposition followed the 'wrong path.' Thus there in their history was waged a continual war between the 'black' yogis and the 'white' yogis.

The object, or goal of the martial artist is to achieve perfect balance, or harmony of the Yin and Yang. Only then is he able to control the life force (Ch'i) with which he believes he can achieve his objectives in overcoming an opponent.

Bob Larson writes, "...The religious and philosophical roots of most martial art forms presuppose a pantheistic perception of the cosmos. Even the curious student runs the risk of being conditioned by the techniques which pursue a goal of impersonal oneness with the universe. The Taoistic and Buddhist overtones represent more than an historical root. These principles are an integral part of fulfilling the ultimate spiritual aim of most (martial) art forms."[11]

The Bible has something to say about this. **"Now the Spirit says expressly that in the latter times people shall depart from the faith, giving heed to seducing spirits, and doctrines of demons," (1 Timothy 4:1).**

Types of Martial Arts

Wado Ryu Karate

Proponents of Karate proclaim that it is *"a self-defence system that utilizes the whole of the human body and the ways in which it moves and twists. Techniques vary from punching and striking with the fist, hands and elbows, to kicks and strikes with the feet, shins and knees."*[12] They further claim, "Karate, whether practiced as an art, sport or as self-defence, carries the motto "never strike the first blow."[12]

Karate means "empty hand," Kara meaning empty and te meaning hand. In other words, fighting with bare hands and feet. It's origins are in the Okinawa Islands of Japan, where people were forbidden to carry weapons. Karate was developed so the local Buddhist monks could protect themselves from bandits while travelling around without using weapons. Although it evolved during the 15th century, its roots can be traced back to ancient India and China. For the better part of 500 years, this form of martial arts was called "Okinawa-te" meaning Okinawa hand. In the early 20th Century, it was amended to Karate-do, or empty hand. Practice of the earlier form was quite violent, with full body contact even during practices. The suffix "do" was added by Yoshitaka Funakoshi as a gentler form, seeking to focus strikes at skin level rather than deliver full blows which would cause significant bruising or broken bones. The goal was to focus more on "physical and spiritual development" rather than those of the warrior.

Taken to mainland Japan in 1905 by Gichin Funakoshi (father of the above-named) Karate was incorporated into the school educational system. Within 20 years, Karate Clubs had begun to be established in Japan's universities. A number of styles of Karate have since developed, and Karate is now one of the most widely practiced forms of martial arts in the world.

There are two main forms of competition in Karate; the Kumite and the

Kata. The Kumite omits certain dangerous techniques for the safety and enjoyability of the competitors, and has a referee or judge. The Kata form is performed alone against imaginary opponents, where points are awarded for correct technique, good balance, timing, rhythm and attitude etc.

Karate users wear a white cotton suit, with a top and trousers. The left side of the top or jacket usually shows the badge of the club the practitioner belongs to. Those doing Karate are expected to remain clean and tidy all the time as a sign of respect to their art, teacher and others doing karate.

There are many different grades in Karate. These are listed here.

Beginners & 10th Kyu wear a White belt

9th kyu = white

8th kyu = white with a yellow strip

7th kyu = yellow

6th kyu = orange

5th kyu = green

4th kyu = blue

3rd kyu = purple

2nd kyu = brown

1st kyu = brown

1st dan = black

(I could but chose not to include this type of information for all the different Martial Arts. This is just to show you the differing grades or levels in this particular form, and similar grades with various colored belts etc. occur in most other Martial Arts.)

Part of the etiquette of Karate is to bow three times prior to a competition. The first bow or Rei is to the Founder or Shomen; the second bow is to the teacher (who is usually positioned in the east); and the third bow is to the competitor.

Shotokan Karate. This claims to be both ancient and young. Ancient because it's roots are deeply entrenched in the past, and young because the main development has been less than 100 years. The man claimed to have founded Shotokan is called Gichan Funakoshi, from Okinawa. He trained in the old system of Okinawan Martial Arts, and brought what he had learned to mainland Japan. The term Shotokan comes from two Japanese terms, shoto meaning waving pines, and kan meaning hall. So it is claimed the name means Shoto's hall of the Way of the Empty Hand. The form we know these days was developed by Funakoshi's son, Yoshitaka. It has grown significantly in popularity. Shotokan Karate uses what are known as triads, metaphors for something much deeper within the human psyche. The physical triad is basics or kihon; sparring or kumite; and forms or Kata. Then there is a moral triad of justice, mercy and compassion and also ethical triad of duty, honour and loyalty. Since nine symbolizes perfection in oriental thinking, these principles are thought to make a well-balanced person.

It is claimed Shotokan develops self-confidence which stimulates wellbeing and an ability to cope with difficult situations. There is also a claim of consciousness of one's environment. It is also believed that the physical development and improvement of technique and ability is useless without this other dimension - the other dimension being compassion and mercy. Like other Karate practitioners, they wear a white cotton top and drawstring trousers, and the belt colours for the different grades differs from that of normal Karate.

A practitioner of Shotokan Karate is called a Karateka. From the third Dan (or grade) they are addressed as Sensei. A Fourth Dan is supposed to be well acquainted with the style and have a deep knowledge of the technical syllabus. The 5th Dan will be awarded when they write a technical thesis on Karate. All Dan grades are for progress with emphasis on style, devotion, dedication and commitment to the art. The Sixth Dan is entitled "The Shihan," which freely translates into "Master" or "Teacher of Teachers." I find it interesting that it is claimed it can take 30 years of hard discipline, training and study to achieve the sixth Dan, and this is also claimed to be the "beginning of the pursuit of excellence." That is a fairly long beginning for a sport.

Part of the etiquette of Shotokan Karate are the three kinds of bow used in differing circumstances. First is the Shomen ni rei, performed as a sign of respect in the training area; there is Otagani rei performed to the great masters of the past and present; and Shihan rei used by both teachers and students.

Aikido

This is an art claimed to teach one how to harmonise or flow with an attack, leading an aggressor to a point of imbalance, and then applying some neutralizing technique. Quite a number of the practitioners believe it is possible to study Aikido as a spiritual discipline alone, learning to unite the spiritual energy - to become "one with nature."

It is also described as a dynamic system of combat. However, it is recognized that Aikido is probably best understood as a mixture of both. Aikido is a reasonable recent innovation developed in Japan in the early 20th century by Morihei Ueshiba (1883 to 1969). He is known to have studied Jujitsu, as well as Kenjitsu and the art of the spear.

Morihei came under the influence of Sokaku Takeda, who was a master of Daito Ryu-aiki jujitsu. That form of Martial Arts had developed around the 6th century and had been used by the military hierarchy and later became known as Oshikiuchi or "striking arts." Morihei later also came under the influence of Onisaburo Deguchi, who was described by supporters as *"the charismatic founder of an esoteric religion called Omoto-Kyo."* Morihei spent six years travelling throughout Asia as Deguchi's disciple.

Morihei named his amalgam of these differing forms into the spiritual beliefs of Ueshiba (his surname) aiko-budo, and finally settled on the name Aikido, because of the meanings of the parts - Ai meaning harmony; Ki meaning spirit; and Do meaning way. (Ki, of course, is the Japanese form of the Taoism's energy or life-force called Ch'i.) Morihei intended participants to harmonize their own spirits with the Spirit of Nature, or the Universal Spirit. As a Martial Art, Aikido is intended *"to harmonize with an attack, lead it to exhaustion and then neutralize it with a throw, joint lock or immobilisation."*[13]

Along with many other martial art forms, there is also the claim not just to be a system of self-defence but also a means of self improvement and spiritual and emotional growth.

According to the founder, the goal of Aikido is not the defeat of others, but the defeat of the negative characteristics which inhibit our own mind and limit its effective functioning. Most of us will be familiar with Yin & Yang concept from traditional Taoism. Aikido thinking is that if you are attacked by a force (the Yang) and you apply force yourself (also Yang) a collision of energies will result in disharmony. This means the strongest Yang force wins. However with Aikido method, the opposing force is first met with Yin movements, which exhaust that Yang force to the point of imbalance. Then Yang force can be applied the Aikido way, to restore harmony and redress the imbalance. So Aikido claims it seeks to harmonise and restrain an opponent, rather than to meet violence with violence.

Weapons are used in Aikido, including a sword (bokken); and a stick (jo) both being used to develop skills and understanding in one-on-one and multiple attack and defence.

All movements by practitioners of Aikido, regardless of their size, weight, strength and age are more to do with learning to use your inner Ki or flow of psychic energy.

There are at least five forms of Aikido practized these days, all of which were created or adapted by men trained by Morihei, but who came away with different ideas of discipline. These forms include Master Gozo Shiodo's Yoshinkan style, Kenji Tomaki's Sport Aikido, Minoru Mochizuki's amalgamated form, and Koichi Tohei's Shin-shin-toitsu Aikido.

Aikido's system has six student grades or kyu's, after which a practitioner may go through the various Dan grades. Apart from children's grades, colored belts are not usual. Men, women and children are all trained together, although certain techniques are not practiced by the children for safety reasons.

Ju Jitsu

Widely used amongst police forces and the military, Ju Jitsu includes defences against knife attacks and teaches how to immobilize an antagonist. There is one interesting skill taught to practitioners of Ju Jitsu, called Kuatsu, which is the art of resuscitation. Having delivered a non-fatal technique rather than a killing blow, a samurai warrior could then revive the injured enemy for questioning.

Let us not forget that Martial also means military. Ju Jitsu translates into Ju, meaning soft or gentle, and Jitsu meaning art. Sometimes this can translate the gentle art or science of softness. There are some who claim Ju Jitsu originated in China, but there are examples on record going back to Japan for this particular art. The Nihon Sho-ki chronicles refer to a martial arts tournament in 23B.C. in the seventh year of the reign of Emperor Shuinjin.

There is also historical evidence of a development of this art by a Buddhist monk around the 13th Century, known as Kumi-tachi. Both the Samurai and Ninja used this form, and it was adopted by many bandits, causing the art to lose its reputation through misuse. Jiguro Kano developed Judo from a combination of Ju Jitsu techniques.

It is claimed the central philosophy behind Ju Jitsu is to conquer an opponent by "all and any means" using a minimum of force. There are strict dietary and moral regimes to be followed by those who want to excel. Many Ju Jitsu masters withdrew to religious institutions, particularly Buddhist and Shinto shrines.

"The Samurai followed a strict code of discipline called the bushido - the "way of the warrior." This code included such concepts as loyalty, duty, obedience, honor and respect. The code influenced not just their behaviour in battle, but their daily lives, too. This would become the basis of the Zen Buddhist philosophy - reaching for salvation within, rather than turning to a monument or god. The Samurai believed that man could influence his own destiny, especially when faced with warfare and possible death - a concept which certainly appealed to them."[14]

The usual uniform for Ju Jitsu is a white suit with a variety of belts - the color showing the grade achieved by the practitioner. The top part of the suit changes to black when the practitioner has reached the 1st Dan level, and changes again to blue on attaining the 4th Dan. Groin protection is compulsory for all participants at all levels - men and women.

Ju Jitsu employs a range of weapons, including:

used for/description	Name
rope (method of restraint)	hojo jutsu
short stick	jo
longer stick	bo
spears	hoko & yari
wooden staff	naginata
small rice flails	nunchaku

Other weapons were developed from agricultural use, such as kamma - a type of rice sickle, and sai, used to ward off sword attacks.

Among the etiquette is respect shown to the spirit of the art called a shomen, and also the instructors, other students and the training environment, called a dojo.

Judo

Judo means the "gentle way." It is a combination of techniques, such as timing and resistance, in which the opponent's body or strength is used against himself. There is some similarity between Judo and sumo wrestling - a small person being more able to overcome a larger opponent. Judo evolved or was developed from Ju Jitsu.

The founder of Judo was Professor Jiguro Kano, a graduate of the Imperial University of Tokyo, Japan. He developed several techniques from Ju Jitsu, and took it to Europe in 1889, where this Martial Art spread quite rapidly. He taught Judo as a life art rather than a sport.

Judo practitioners, known as Judoka, wear a Judogi (a heavy cotton jacket and trousers), and hold competitions in a judojo (hall). In Western Judo two main attitudes are expected from Judoka: 1) a state of permanent alertness. 2) demonstrating control and discipline over the mind and the body. These enable Judoka to have trained responses to every situation.

Kano was the first to train women in any Martial Art, and despite coming under some criticism for doing so, he established a training hall or dojo just for women in Tokyo.

Kano felt strongly that Judo was a personal art to train the mind and body, but he never created it to be a public competition sport. Kano stated "Judo is the means of understanding the way to make the most effective use of both physical and spiritual power and strength. By devoted practice and rigid discipline, in an effort to obtain perfection in attacking and defending, it refines the body and soul and helps instil the spiritual essence in Judo into every part of one's very being. In this way, it is possible to perfect oneself and contribute something worthwhile to the world."[15]

This is an interesting statement from a man who clearly developed Judo as a spiritual exercise, apart from it's other uses in his life. While this is a common Eastern way of thinking, it reaffirms the spiritual basis common to all Eastern Martial Arts, as well as the frequently obvious claim to spiritual transformation some call salvation by ones-self. What is sold to the Western world as a health, fitness and self-esteem-building art, is actually a form of spiritual salvation without a savior, apart from self.

Kung Fu

Kung fu means "a sustained effort or skill," and incorporates hundreds of styles. Some are listed below.

Wing Chun.

Ng Mui, the woman who founded Wing Chun, is alleged to have observed a battle between a snake and a crane. She mimicked those fighting movements in this Martial Art.

She developed a close-quarter combat system completely different to contemporary practices. She discarded many of the traditional ways, which frequently required many years of practice at every stage. Her system is based on the principle of winning at all cost, by using speed and flexibility to overcome the natural advantages of an opponent.

"The emphasis lay in sudden contraction and relaxation causing the practitioner to explode into action using natural weapons such as finger jabs to the eyes, elbow strikes to the face, and the powerful use of knees and feet to an opponent's lower body." [16]

"Subsequent generations of Wing Chun practitioners have refined the system further, but always keeping to the simple, almost scientific, principles of the art: the centre line theory (protecting and striking at the major pressure points); economy of motion (keeping every movement as simple as possible); and the self- explanatory principle of combined or simultaneous defence and attack." [16]

"Wing chun is centred on the Taoist principle of take the middle road. In essence, this says that you should not go to extremes, and that success is based on balance." [16.]

Mok Gar

Shaolin Mok-Gar Kuen comes from southern China, and is well-known for its kicking techniques drawn from the disciplines of Kung Fu. This form of martial arts also uses a full range of weapons as well as kicking. Along with other forms of martial arts it incorporates both attack and defence and seeks and expresses triumph in combat. Shaolin Mok Gar Kuen was originally developed by a very short man named Mok-Da-Si. He was based in the Shaolin monastery in Kwong-Tong province. This form has remained virtually unchanged for many generations, and practice usually involves the use of two wooden dummies. One has projections which resemble arms, and in practice is used for blocking and countering; the second consists of a hollow bamboo post about 4 m high and 10 cm in diameter, (13 feet by 4 inches) and it's filled with washers or coins for students to practice their attacks on. This form of training helps build physical power and develops effective punches and kicks.

Tae Kwon Do

This form of martial arts is believed to have been developed by a Buddhist monk named Won Qwang. There are five principles

in Tae Kwon Do. These include etiquette, modesty, perseverance, self-control, and indomitable or invincible spirit. It is widely known for its exceptional kicking and jumping techniques. Taught and practiced as a sport, it is also promoted as an effective self defence system. Some of the training relates to karate, with simple punching and blocking techniques. Tae Kwon Do has developed from a number of martial arts, but the main influence is Korean Kickfighting, Tae-Kyon.

Although Tae Kwon Do's roots go back over 2000 years, where it was originally known as Hwarang Do, meaning the way of the flowering manhood; modern Tae Kwon Do was developed in Korea in the 1950's. Major General Choi Hong Hi is thought to be the founder, having a 9th dan black belt. The major influence in this form of martial arts was Confucian teaching, particularly during the Silla dynasty around 680. The Silla kingdom was the smallest of the three on the Korean peninsula, being constantly attacked by its two stronger neighbors. Because of this, their leaders developed a fighting system to protect themselves. Between the 10th and 16 century, Tae Kwon Do became compulsory for young men of military age. When military traditions declined after the 16th century, Tae Kwon Do was kept alive by the local Buddhist monks. All forms of Martial Arts were suppressed during the Japanese occupation, which began in 1909. However, some practitioners escaped to China, and took Tae Kwon Do with them.

The name Tae Kwon Do means "to connect or smash with the feet"; "to intercept or strike with the hands." The purpose of this martial art is to overcome an attacker swiftly, by using both hands and feet. Tae Kwon Do has a variety of disciplines including Kung Fu, Kyokushinkai karate, Thai boxing and Kokky Shinkai.

During the 1970's, when there was a boom in martial arts in the West, many styles of martial arts fighting, particularly in Britain and America began to take on a more westernised form. Some claim that

during this time, America became the source of kickboxing. This is thought to have occurred because American karate practitioners were becoming frustrated with the limitations of tournament scoring. Great emphasis is placed on kicks and punches with full force. Part of the evolution of Kickboxing was the development of weight divisions similar to normal boxing. Safety rules developed, including protective clothing, because of the high risk of injury. The protective clothing, includes a head guard, gum shield, groin guard shin, hand and foot pads. Women usually wear the same except the groin guard is swapped for a chest guard. There are women's competitions, but generally, they do not compete against men.

Tae Kwon Do has been an Olympic sport since 1988. Competitions have three main sections: sparring, patterns and destruction. In sparring, the aim is to score points through the delivery of correct techniques at target areas. Timing, focus and speed are key elements. In the patterns section, a specified series of combination techniques is performed against an imaginary opponent in a sequential order. Karate elements are included. In the destruction section, practitioners display techniques to break pieces of wood, bricks, and so on. Experts so focuse their minds that, aided by psychic power, they can easily break objects humanly impossible to break. Furthermore, they sustain no personal injury.

Kendo

This is a very fast striking martial art, and often involves high-pitched screams. Kendo derives from the ancient Japanese samurai sword fighting. Protective armor is worn. The sword is made of four sections of bamboo bound together to create what is called a shinai.

Kenjitsu dates prior to 1590 and developed into the modern Kendo. The shinai was a safer way to practice swordsmanship than with real blades. Wooden replicas of swords, called bokken and a practice sword called

katana are used. Although people of many walks of life may be involved in Kendo these days, traditionally it was limited to the samurai, also known as Bushi. One of Japan's most famous swordsman was Musashi Miyamoto (1584-1645), who made an interesting statement when he said "To win the battle is to be prepared to die."

Speed and body movements are very important in the delivery of skilful technique. Mental and physical control are claimed to be of utmost importance . The balance of the two leads to harmony, not only in the art, but in your general wellbeing. There are four very deep mental hurdles, which must be overcome; fear, doubts, surprise and confusion. These are known as "the four poisons of Kendo."

Iaido

This is another sword-based Martial Arts where the aim is to draw your sword and strike an armed opponent at lightning speed. "Live blades are razor sharp and experienced practitioners are the only ones permitted to use them. The risk involved is thought worthwhile, because this is the only way to achieve the ultimate in awareness and concentration, and to bring mind and body together in total harmony."[17]

Iaido comes from the ancient way of the samurai warrior and is thought to date from around 400 AD. The sword for practice is called a bokken, and is a solid wooden stick, usually made from red or white oak. Part of the art is the drawing of the sword from the scabbard. The blade was long and straight, and the Japanese warrior would carry it on his left side. Many used these days are not the traditional Japanese sword because they are curved. Although it is a separate martial art, Iaido is closely related to Kendo. While Kendo requires two people facing each other, Iaido is for individuals. It involves a series of set movements in which the sword is drawn, and an imaginary opponent is cut. The sword is then resheathed. It is claimed the ultimate purpose of Iaido is to overcome your enemy without having to draw your sword by conquering your opponent spiritually and without having to resort to violence. One of their quotations is insightful. “Your mind is not disturbed by you being beaten up, but by you, beating up others.”

Many of the techniques of Iaido are related to Zen Buddhist practice. A 15th century of Zen sword master, Yagyu Munenori, developed the concept of “the unfettered mind,” which means remaining calm in the face of adversity.

Hayashizaki Jinnosuke Shigenobo founded a martial art school called Iai Jutsu in 1560. By the late 1960's Iaido was unified with all the various styles involving swords.

Shinto Ryu

Shinto means shrine. Shinto Ryu means 'spirit of nature' or 'nature's way.' It is claimed to be a street defence strategy, useful for all, irrespective of age, fitness and gender. It is sold to young people to deal with bullying.

In Shinto Ryu, various martial art styles have been blended into two techniaues: 1) hard or forceful self-defence, and 2) soft, accepting, deflective movements. Faced with unsolicited or threatening situations, the practitioner can chose either method and is able to respond to a progression of physical violence. Trusting our intuition is an important element. Objects at hand, such as chairs or small tables are used both as barriers and part of the self-defence strategy. A bamboo stick is also included in the practice is a replica of a potential weapon.

Tai Ch'i Chuan

Tai Ch'i Chuan is believed to have originated with Chang San Feng, who was born around 1247. He studied at the famous Shaolin Temple mastering its method of martial arts. He traveled from there to the Wutang mountains, where there are a large number of Taoist hermits. It is believed that he watched a stork and snake fight and seeing the fluidity of their movements developed Tai Ch'i. It is also claimed that Chang became expert at striking his opponents' acupuncture points.

Tai Ch'i Chuan is translated into English as "The supreme ultimate first." The term Chuan refers to boxing with an empty hand. Every form of Tai Ch'i Chuan I have seen advertised boasts that it is based on Chinese Taoist philosophies. It is also referred to as "internal kung fu." This means it has more to do with spiritual breathing exercises, flexibility and mind rather than muscular strength.

Tai Ch'i Chuan makes no apology for the use of the Yin and Yang principles which are described elsewhere. It is claimed that Tai Ch'i Chuan is a method of "serene movements for health and wellbeing with a strong fighting system of self-defence"[18] Tai Ch'i has also been called "Chinese Yoga".

Another name associated with Tai Ch'i Chuan was Yang Lu Chan (1799-1872). Yang was undefeated, despite many challengers, and was instructed to teach the imperial family and their bodyguards.

A more recent style called Wing Chun Kuen Kung Fu is attributed to a woman named Yim Wing Chun, who was the protégé of a Buddhist nun, Ng Mui. Wing Chun means 'beautiful springtime', and Kuen means 'fist or fighting style.' Known as a soft style of Martial Arts, Wing Chun actually has a blend of both hard and soft techniques.

During the 1920's Tai Ch'i Chuan began to spread throughout China.

The health benefits became recognized and were adopted as a national exercise. Tai Ch'i Chuan has spread to the West since the 1960's, and is claimed to be the most widely practised martial art in the world.

After almost 35 years of Japanese occupation and with the return of many Korean exiles following World War II, Tae Kwon Do became part of the Korean national identity. It was brought to the West, after the 1950's, by servicemen returning to America and other allied nations.

The form of today's Tai Ch'i Chuan includes punches, kicks, locks, open-hand techniques and a number of traditional Chinese weapons, including sword, broadsword, staff and spear. It is claimed to be one of the best antidotes to stress in the Western world.

One of the primary claims of Tai Ch'i Chuan is to teach relaxation. This means absence of muscular tension, not flopping loosely. Good posture with relaxed shoulders is required, along with an upright back and a stance which is firmly rooted. Deep breathing exercises and quiet concentration are requirements for Tai Ch'i Chuan. The stresses of life are claimed to be placed in the proper perspective. Exercises called Ch'i Kung must be practiced to strengthen the body first before the martial arts form of Tai Ch'i Chuan can be developed. It is claimed to be an excellent self-defence method where practitioners relax and develop fluid movements.

Andrew McIntosh wrote, "Tai Ch'i Chuan is derived from three sources.

1. Collective Chinese Philosophies.

2. Shaolin martial arts.

3. The Study of nature.

If we break this down further we discover three major principles upon which Tai Ch'i is based.

I Ching (The book of Changes) is considered by Tai Ch'i proponents to be an important divination manual from which the most basic principles of Tai Ch'i have been derived. In other words it seems fair to conclude that the foundation from which the most basic and fundamental principles of Tai Ch'i were derived was divination.

The Yin and Yang, previously referred to, developed from the study of superstition, divination, and spirituality. As we delve further into the philosophy of the Yin and Yang we will see it's strong link to witchcraft.

The five elements. Ancient Chinese conceived that everything in the world belonged to one of five elements wood, metal, water, fire, and earth. These five elements represented tangible components, or creations of Yin and Yang.

It seems reasonable to conclude that divination is the common link between the three major principles upon which Tai Ch'i is founded.

Taoism and Tai Ch'i are also very closely linked as Taoist breathing techniques and meditation techniques are incorporated into Tai Ch'i. A brief summation of Taoism shows that it has three main sources.

Pantheism the belief that God is everything. i.e. I am God, you are God, everyone and everything is God. However, the Bible emphatically rejects this notion see John 17:3 "And this is life eternal that they may know you, the only true God, and Jesus Christ whom you have sent". There are many other verses of scripture that ratify this vital truth.

The philosophies of Lao Tse. The Bible warns of such philosophies in Colossians 2:8 "See to it that no-one takes you captive through hollow and deceptive philosophy, which depends on human tradition and the basic principles of this world rather than on Christ."

Sorcery. Divination through the assistance of evil spirits; black magic; enchantment; & witchcraft. (See Leviticus 19:26, and Deuteronomy 18:10-12.)[19]

Some, who are either sincerely ignorant of the philosophy behind Tai Ch'i, or who have a hidden agenda, falsely claim it is just a physical exercise. However, the major writings about Tai Ch'i claim you cannot practice it without the philosophy behind it having a significant meaning in your life. The primary goal of Tai Ch'i is to reach the Tan Tien - the psychic centre of the soul which is claimed by Taoists to be located 7 cm below the navel. It is claimed this is where the Ch'i is stored, so the Yin and Yang may be kept in balance.

Since part of the Tai Ch'i process is to empty the mind of conscious thought, there is an inherent danger in doing that. While this is covered further in the TM section below, emptying one's mind creates a vacuum which thereby allows the psychic or evil spiritual realm to infiltrate and play with your spirit and soul. Any person who empties their mind

gives control over it to someone or something else. Mind-emptying meditation, hypnosis and other psychic practices should be avoided by anyone who really wants to remain spiritually, emotionally and physically healthy. From my own experience, hypnosis is the tool of choice for those who don't have a relationship with the Holy Spirit of God. Under the guise of Tai Ch'i, this allows the demons/evil spirits to gain entry to the psychic or divination centre of the soul, resulting in demonization.

"The apocryphal founder of Tai Ch'i was a monk of the Wu Tang Monastery, Chang San-feng to whom have been ascribed various dates and longevities. Some scholars doubt his historical existence, viewing him as a literary construct! Other research and records from the Ming-shih (the official chronicles of the Ming dynasty) seem to indicate that he lived in the period from 1391 to 1459 (he may have been born earlier and lived later: these are simply some dates associated with him).

Linking some of the older forms with the notion of Yin-Yang from Taoism and stressing the 'internal' aspects of his exercises, he is credited with creating the fundamental 'Thirteen Postures' of Tai Ch'i corresponding to the eight basic trigrams of the I Ching and the five elements.

The eight 'postures' are:

ward-off

rollback

press

push

pull

split

elbow strike;

shoulder strike

The five 'attitudes' are:

advance

retreat

look left

gaze right;

central equilibrium.

His exercises stressed suppleness and elasticity and were opposed to hardness and force. They incorporated philosophy, physiology, psychology, geometry and the laws of dynamics.

Wang Chung-yueh, and his student Chiang Fa elaborated his theories, writings, and practices sometime later. Wang apparently took the thirteen postures of Chang San-feng and linked them together into continuous sequences, thus creating something which resembles the contemporary Tai Ch'i Chuan form. His student Chiang Fa taught Tai Ch'i to the villagers of a town on Honan (almost all of whom were called Chen) and thus began the first family school of Tai Chi Chuan.

Where do the teachings of Tai Ch'i ultimately lead? To answer this question lets hear what the teachings of Tai Ch'i have to say. *"By utilizing the principles of the I Ching in order, the practitioner is allowed to pass through the state of tranquillity to ultimately enter the fourth dimension. One living in the fourth dimension is really a god who knows the past, present, and future. This goal is also known as ultimate enlightenment. So the ultimate lie of Tai Ch'i is that we can be as God."*[20]

Transcendental Meditation

TM was founded by Maharishi Mahesh Yogi in 1958. He moved to the United States of America in 1961. Maharishi probably thought he had "made it" with the "conversion" of The Beatles music group.

Maharishi stated that TM's goal is to permanently alter the meditator's perception of the world until it harmonises with the Hindu pantheistic world view. The United States Federal Court legally identified TM as a religion in 1976, which was upheld by the Court of Appeal in 1979. "The entire mission of TM is to counter the ever spreading demon of Christianity," according to a senior spokesperson for TM in India in 1981.

In a brochure published by the Maharishi Foundation of New Zealand Inc., there is an interesting statement saying *"TM is taught by an international, charitable, non-profit, non-religious, educational organization."* It goes on to state *"TM is not a lifestyle, a religion, a system of belief or a philosophy; TM does not involve a change in your beliefs or lifestyle."* This seems inconsistent with the establishment of the parent organization as a religion in the USA.

Christians and non-Christians alike were encouraged to practice this form of meditation as a relief from stress, to lower blood pressure, improve mental health, improve their sex life and much more. While these may seem laudable, TM's promoters have been dishonestly saying things like *"It's not a religion,"* and *"It's a technique which won't interfere with your own beliefs or lack of beliefs, your life style or your job. It's so beneficial, just a few minutes a day repeating the mantra will enable you to transcend all your troubles, and you will have peace, joy, good health..."* and so on.

These are not only bold claims - thousands who have tried TM have found it is simply not true. TM is usually taught as a non-religious meditation. This is blatantly untrue - it is straight Hinduism dressed up for the Western world as a "technique" rather than a religion.

If TM isn't a religion, why is Guru Dev's photo bowed down to in worship at every initiation?

If TM isn't a religion, why are seventeen different items (including handkerchiefs, flowers and fruit) all offered to the various Hindu deities named in the ceremony? These are acts of homage and worship.

In effect, many thousands of people, in ignorance, have actually become Hindus by their active participation in the initiation and worship ceremonies of TM.

If TM was honest, why aren't initiates provided with a copy of the initiation ceremony in their mother tongue prior to going through it?

The English translation of its Initiatory Puja or ritual prayer, clearly states that the person is bowing down to over fourteen different Hindu deities, and the teacher Guru Dev is bowed down to as deity (seventeen times in the second part). This Puja is simply a hymn of worship in Sanskrit.

People are refused an English language copy of what they are saying prior to or during their initiation. I wonder how many people have been tricked into this idolatry? Any Christian practicing

TM is jeopardizing their salvation, and should repent and leave it immediately. Many have come out and having rejected it, have stated that TM's claims are largely illusory, its results are mostly unhealthy and it is deceptive at every level.

TM's Initiatory Puja

(This has been translated from the Sanskrit and a direct quote from their own teaching manual) [21]

"Invocation

Whether pure or impure, whether purity or impurity is permeating everywhere, whoever opens himself to the expanded vision of unbounded awareness gains inner and outer purity.

To Lord Narayana, to lotus-born Brahma the Creator, to Vashishtha, to Shakti and his son Parashar, to Vyasa, to Shukadeva, to the great Caudapada, to Govinda, ruler among the yogis, to his disciple, Shri Shankarachaya, to his disciples Padma Pada and Hasta Malaka and Trotakacharya, and Vartikakara, to others, to the tradition of our Masters, I bow down.

To the abode of the wisdom of the Shrutis, Smritis and Puranas, to the abode of kindness, to the personified glory of the Lord, to Shankara, emancipator of the world, I bow down.

To Shankaracharya the redeemer, hailed as Krishna and Badarayna, to the commentator of the Brahmasutras, I bow down. To the glory of the Lord I

bow down again and again, at whose door the whole galaxy of gods pray for perfection day and night.

Adorned with immeasurable glory, preceptor of the whole world, having bowed down to Him we gain fulfilment.

Skilled in dispelling the cloud of ignorance of the people, the gentle emancipator, Brahmananda Sarasvati, the supreme teacher, full of brilliance, Him I bring to my awareness.

Offering the invocation to the lotus feet of Shri Guru Dev, I bow down.

Offering a seat to the lotus feet of Shri Guru Dev, I bow down.

Offering an ablution of the lotus feet of Shri Guru Dev, I bow down.

Offering cloth to the lotus feet of Shri Guru Dev, I bow down.

Offering sandlepaste to the lotus feet of Shri Guru Dev, I bow down.

Offering full rice to the lotus feet of Shri Guru Dev, I bow down.

Offering a flower to the lotus feet of Shri Guru Dev, I bow down.

Offering incense to the lotus feet of Shri Guru Dev, I bow down.

Offering light to the lotus feet of Shri Guru Dev, I bow down.

Offering water to the lotus feet of Shri Guru Dev, I bow down.

Offering fruit to the lotus feet of Shri Guru Dev, I bow down.

Offering a betel leaf to the lotus feet of Shri Guru Dev, I bow down.

Offering a coconut to the lotus feet of Shri Guru Dev, I bow down.

Offering a Camphor Light

White as camphor, kindness incarnate, the essence of creation garlanded with Brahman, ever dwelling in the lotus of my heart, the creative impulse of cosmic life, to That, in the form of Guru Dev, I bow down.

Offering light to the lotus feet of Shri Guru Dev, I bow down.

Offering water to the lotus feet of Shri Guru Dev, I bow down.

Offering a Handful of Flowers

Guru, in the glory of Brahma, Guru, in the glory of Vishnu, Guru, in the glory of the great Lord Shiva, Guru, in the glory of the personified transcendental fullness of Brahman, to Him, to Shri Guru Dev adorned with glory, I bow down.

The unbounded, like the endless canopy of the sky, the omnipresent in all creation, by whom the sign of That has been revealed, to Him, to Shri Guru Dev, I bow down.

Guru Dev, Shri Brahmananda, bliss of the Absolute, transcendental joy, the Self-Sufficient, the embodiment of pure knowledge which is beyond and above the universe like the sky, the aim of "Thou Art

That" and other such expressions which unfold eternal truth, the One, the Eternal, the Pure, the Immoveable, the Witness of all intellects, whose status transcends thought, the Transcendent along with the three gunas, the true preceptor, to Shri Guru Dev, I bow down.

The blinding darkness of ignorance has been removed by applying the balm of knowledge. The eye of knowledge has been opened to Him, and therefore, to Him, to Shri Guru Dev, I bow down. Offering a handful of flowers to the lotus feet of Shri Guru Dev, I bow down."

Comment:

The initiation ritual is the most important stage in learning and practising TM The heart of the ritual is the Puja, (a Sanskrit hymn of worship) shown above. These are accompanied by physical movements which accompany the recitation. Following these words there is the impartation of a Mantra - the secret word on which to meditate. This Puja is never given to the initiate in English, even when it is asked for. The only people with access to these words within TM are those trained personally and exclusively by Maharishi, The primary purpose of this special training is so they may initiate others.

There are three phases in the ceremony of Initiation. The first is a recitation of various beings of myth, legend and history believed to represent the "apostolic succession" of the TM holy tradition, beginning with Hindu mythology and ending with Maharishi's own spiritual master, Brahmananda Sarasvati, otherwise known as Guru Dev. Each person named in this phase of the puja is regarded not merely as a human being, but as a fully realized expression of divinity, according to Brooks Alexander. *"All are exalted as deities worthy of worship."*[22]

The second phase of the Puja places offerings before the image of Guru Dev along with the words, as an act of worship. (For Scriptures which forbid this, see Jeremiah 18:15; 1 Corinthians 8:4; & 10:28)

The third phase is nothing other than *"a hymn of praise and adoration to Guru Dev as deity."*[22]

Only after following all three steps in this initiation is the initiate given their "Mantra." A Mantra is a word or series of words which the initiate must repeat over and over again, until they enter or transcend into an altered state of consciousness, or trancelike state. This spiritual state will often involve a visit by a spirit guide, which will often have the name of the mantra. Spirit guides are elsewhere called evil spirits of demons, and the mantra is usually its name.

Those of us used to ministering in this area helping people deal with such spirits, can attest that involvement in Witchcraft, Wicca, Spiritualism and more are actually putting themselves in deep jeopardy by that involvement. TM is clearly related spiritually to these through this practice. People who take mind-altering drugs often report having a similar experience with these spirit guides.

Meditation which empties the mind allows for spirit guides to come and fill the mind with other junk. This would be a fairly quick way to a mental disorder caused by a demon. Genuine meditation involves contemplating on the positive promises recorded in God's Word, the Holy Bible, rather than creating a vacuum for a demon to fill.

Three brief but vital points need to be made.

1. Our meditation must be acceptable to God:

"Let the words of my mouth and the meditation of my heart be acceptable in Your sight, O Lord, my strength and my Redeemer." (Psalm 19:14)

2. We need the Word of God in our hearts before we can meditate effectively.

"I will meditate on Your precepts, and contemplate Your ways. I will delight myself in Your statutes; I will not forget Your word." (Psalm 119:15-16)

3. Meditation is the time to review what our minds have been taught.

"This Book of the Law shall not depart from your mouth, but you shall meditate in day and night, that you may observe to do according to all that is written in it. For then, you will make your way prosperous, and then you will have good success." (Joshua 1:8)

It is impossible to meditate our way into a relationship with God. However, we must approach God His way, and the only way He will accept us is through Jesus Christ. **"For there is one God and one Mediator between God and man, the Man Christ Jesus, who**

gave Himself a ransom for many, to be testified in due time." (1 Timothy. 2:5-6).

Too many have settled for counterfeit and temporary peace when they could have had - and still can have - the genuinely real peace only God our creator can provide through Jesus Christ.

Throughout all this, the elements of worship to both Hindu deities as well as human deities or living gods is very evident. There can be no doubt this is Hinduism dressed up as something else. It seeks to appeal to ignorant Westerners, from whom the idolatry is kept until they are too deeply involved to care. The main purpose of involvement in TM is to produce an altered state of consciousness, allowing mind control over both the teacher and the candidate for initiation.
Visualization/Guided Imagery

This is attempting to conjure up in our minds a particular, perhaps painful, episode in our past. God is well able to bring to a person a vision or memory if He chooses. But the use of suggestion by a counsellor talking their way through some imagined scene is not a Christian option. This is attempting to use Jesus as a "Spirit Guide." All Christian counselors should prayerfully point us to God who does meet the needs of the emotionally hurt. It is also important to use our wills to forgive. Roy Livesey said *"Believers in Jesus Christ walk in faith. Believing is not the same as imagining or visualising which are neither taught nor encouraged anywhere in Scripture. However visualising is well understood by those familiar with the occult realm."*[23] God may and does give visions, etc., but we would be wise to leave their instigation to Him. Attempting to create a false reality in our own minds and imaginations has proved dangerous and damaging to many people.

Yoga

The word Yoga comes from the Sanskrit 'Yo' and 'ga' - meaning Man and God. The aim is to bring union between them. Like TM, it is based firmly in Hinduism and every aspect has a spiritual purpose, despite claims to the contrary by those who are hiding the truth, or are ignorant of it. Yoga's basic belief is that the spiritual body is held in bondage to the physical body, and the Yogic posturing is supposed to manipulate the skeletal and muscular structure in order to release the spiritual body for union with the God-force.

"There is no Yoga without Hinduism, it is the highest form - the very heart of it. The hope of immortality is Yoga," says an advanced Yoga instructor. The exercises are designed to move the SERPENT FORCE of KHUNDALINI (the name of the demon) up the spine to the brain, and manifest in the so-called "third eye" in the centre of the forehead. The Bhagavadgita says Yoga is the way out of the reincarnation cycle. This is confirmed by Rabi Maharaj, a former Hindu Brahmin priest who is now a true Christian, - *"You can't have yoga without Hinduism, and you can't have Hinduism without yoga"!*[24]

There are several types of Yoga, with differing but complementary purposes. Most people in the western world have seen advertising for Hatha Yoga - the so-called physical exercise. This is taught as a physical exercise in many places we wouldn't normally associate with Hindu religious matters, including the YMCA and even some churches (who must be ignorant of what it truly involves). The fact remains that Yoga is bound up into Hindu religious metaphysics.

All Yoga postures (called asanas) are an integral part of Raja or royal Yoga, also known as Ashtanga or eight-limbed Yoga. Philosophically the body is believed to be just a crude layer of mind, and as such, consciousness needs to influence the body.

"Asana (physical postures) is indispensable as one of the eight stages of Raja Yoga because the yoga postures are themselves specifically designed

to manipulate consciousness, to a greater or lesser degree, into Raja Yoga's consummate experience of Samadhi: undifferentiated union with the primal essence of consciousness, the monist's equivalent of "God"[25].

Writing about Asanas, Swami Vivikananda states *"A series of exercises, physical and mental, is to be gone through every day until certain higher states are reached. Nerve currents will have to be displaced and given a new channel. New sorts of vibrations will begin: the whole constitution will be remodelled, as it were."*[26]

Hatha Yoga has almost always been understood in much the same way as Raja Yoga. One of the classic texts on Hatha Yoga states emphatically *"Having thus solemnly saluted his master Yogi Svatmarama now presents Hatha Vidya (vidya means "wisdom") solely and exclusively for the attainment of Raja Yoga. For those who wander in the darkness of conflicting creeds, unable to reach to the heights of Raja Yoga, the merciful Svatmarama has lit the torch of Hatha Wisdom."*[27]

It must be obvious to anyone who can read that Hatha Yoga is to prepare a person's consciousness for the more subtle metaphysics of Raja Yoga. Regardless of what the Hatha Yoga practitioner believes, Hatha is regarded as a *"torch to experimentally guide one from that belief into the "wisdom" of Raja Yoga."*[24] Alain Danielou, a recognized French scholar on Yoga wrote "The sole purpose for the physical practices of Hatha Yoga is to suppress physical obstacles on the Spiritual or Royal path of Raja Yoga; and Hatha Yoga is therefore called "the ladder to Raja Yoga."[28]

The usual Hindu commentaries on Yoga warn of dire consequences if Hatha Yoga is relegated to just another form of physical exercise. *"Indeed, from the practice of Hatha Yoga, with a proper effort to discipline the mind... mental and spiritual degeneration may ultimately occur,"* according to the Ananda Marga Yoga Society's training manual for teachers.[29]

How Yoga Works

"The typical middle-class Westerner, taking yoga classes at the WMCA, has little or no idea of the how's and why's of yoga's seemly efficacy. In the traditional understanding, physical yoga has a great deal more to do with the practitioner's invisible, "subtle" body, than it does with the flesh and bones and muscles which encase it. While yoga does purport to first of all work on the muscular, glandular and physical nervous systems, it's real import, as Danielou says, is a "process of control of the gross body which aims at freeing the subtle body."[28] This subtle body is extremely complex, but can be superficially described as consisting of 72,000 invisible psychic channels called nadis, which constitute an other-dimensional body which directly corresponds to the physical or gross body.

"The subtle body is connected to the gross body at several points, with the seven predominant ones located at distinct points ranging from the base of the spine to the top of the head. These are called chakras, and they are believed to control the various aspects of the consciousness of the individual. Physical yoga finds it's most refined expression when it teaches postures which bring various channels within the subtle body into a specific alignment with one another, and thus alter the consciousness of the practitioner in a specified way."[25]

This article went on to state: *"Whether or not this sort of thing is actually going on (and there seems no solid Biblical reason for saying it's not) it is important to understand that physical yoga, according to it's classical definitions, is inherently and functionally incapable of being separated from Eastern religious metaphysics. The Western practitioner who attempts to do so is operating in ignorance and danger, from the yogi's viewpoint, as well as from the Christian's."*

In summary, this all means there are spiritual dangers for anyone attempting Yoga, and there are potential emotional and demonic issues which should be avoided by anyone who really wants to please the God who created them.

Jnana Yoga

This is described as, *"...putting an emphasis on knowledge, not just any knowledge, but insight into those eternal laws which lie beneath the surface facts of life. The student must polish his mind until it becomes a perfect mirror for the whole universe - the seen and the unseen ... for one who has an inclination toward science and philosophy, the yoga of wisdom through knowledge will have most appeal."*[30]

Bhakti Yoga

This is "known as 'the way of devotion.' Bhakti Yoga majors on love and the surrender of self to the Supreme Spirit. This supreme spirit may be an 'incarnation of the god-head such as Krishna, (many yogis believe that Christ and Krishna are one and the same) a god realized man, or a mental image of a personal god. This is the way for those of a 'devotional nature' who they say find joy in being able to lose themselves in 'adoration to the Supreme Being." This 'Supreme Being' is spoken of as the 'Light Bearer,' or 'Carrier of Light,' whom they unashamedly refer to as Lucifer! He is of course, none other than the Devil himself!"[31]

Karma Yoga

This is the 'path of action' and is supposedly the way for people who are 'moved by a passionate sympathy for the suffering and want to do something about it.' The understanding given by the Theosophical Society in Sydney (Australia) for this form of yoga was, quote, *"..Mother Theresa would be a prime example of someone giving their whole life to Karma Yoga. She would be practicing Bhakti Yoga in her devotional life, but primarily she would be a practitioner of Karma Yoga."* Notice how subtly and how appealing are the explanations of the 'web weavers' of deceit, who are setting enticing traps for the unwary![31]

Raja Yoga

Raja Yoga is known as the 'Royal Road' and is often described as a 'Kingly Science.' Hatha Yoga is part and parcel of Raja Yoga. This form is said by many devotees to be the highest form of Yoga, hence the name Raja, meaning royal. However, many will dispute that their form of yoga is the highest form, e.g. the Hare Krishna people say that Bhakti Yoga is the ultimate way of achieving Krishna Consciousness. [31]

What about Pilates?

Pilates was developed by Joseph Pilates, a German who moved to England in 1912. As a hospital orderly he was faced with many First World War disabled casualties. He designed a series of 34 exercises to aid muscle strengthening and stretching. These exercises also improved posture, aligned the body, increased strength and helped many avoid further injury. While the postures are simply aerobic and beneficial, some who teach Yoga and other exercise postures which have a spiritual/occultic basis behind them have adopted Pilates. This in part is because it has become so popular, and there is money to be made from teaching it. Care should be taken to avoid trainers who have sought to merge Pilates into their occultic philosophy and practices.

What should we do about all this?

There needs to be a recognition that none of what we have been looking at here is pleasing to God. On that solid understanding, there then needs to be repentance for involvement, either personally, or inherited iniquity through parents etc. who were involved in these practices, and for which the person is paying in health and other ways.

There will be evil spirits which need their legal grounds removed through repentance to God, and then through the ministry of deliverance, freedom should be obtained. I often use the illustration of a landfill or rubbish dump to explain a key issue here. Rats are a common inhabitant at rubbish dumps. They are there because there is food to eat - even if we humans wouldn't eat it. If the food part of the rubbish was removed and not replaced, the rats would quickly get hungry, go looking elsewhere for something to eat. Demons are like those rats. They hang around people because there is something for them to chew on - us! Jesus called them "Unclean" and "Evil." That shows their character and nature - they are unclean and seek to influence us to become involved in acts of uncleaness - spiritually or sexually. They are the primary influences why people get involved in the occult, including witchcraft, wicca, spiritualism, Freemasonry and much more. Their task is our destruction, and their method is to make evil look so good we'll have a go at it. Because humans often have inherited spiritual blindness, we have a tendency to dive straight into wrongdoing without thinking about the consequences - or even being aware there are any.

I doubt I can be surprised by matters people bring up when they want to be set free in ministry. What people have done to each other, and to animals, is disgusting, sad, dehumanizing and very damaging. I am not a demon-hunter. I have never had the intention of lifting every rock to see if a demon lurks under it. However, if I see a demon sitting on the rock, I'm going to reach for a spiritual baseball bat and send it to its appointed place to await judgement from the Lord Jesus. If the person is repentant of those things which have granted a demon permission to afflict them, then ministry is going to be quite easy. The person should be set free in a matter of minutes. I used to think we had to wrestle with the demons like pigs in a mud wallow, often for hours before the person was set free. No more! If the person isn't repentant, then nothing will shift the demon. If they are repentant, then freedom should come swiftly. Actually the demons would love us to wrestle with them like the pig - because it will wear us out, we may give up before we achieve their eviction (through our ignorance); and we still end up with mud on us, so to speak. There is also the probability that other people will hear about such lengthy wrestling matches, decide they would rather keep the demon/s than have that sort of ministry inflicted on their "dignity"

A Christian friend (who often ministers into this area with people who want to be spiritually cleaned up and set free) mentioned to me recently that Siddatha Gautama, the 'Buddha,' abandoned Hinduism because of its idols, yet the followers of Buddha have made an idol out of him.

I recall a phone conversation I had with a former Buddhist monk from Thailand who had since become a Christian and renounced all the occult stuff involved. This brother said he remembered Buddha's writings. Buddha stated that he was not a god, but people would recognize the true God when they saw a man walking on water. Considering this was written about 500 years prior to Jesus Christ, this is insightful at least.

We need to deal with Kali, the Hindu serpent goddess of Death and Destruction. This is a demonic principality whose intention is the person's ultimate destruction. There are also likely to be strongholds from spirits of Death, Murder and Violence - among others.

NOTE: If you have practiced Yoga, Martial Arts of any kind, Transcendental Meditation, other Hindu meditations or chants (including Hare Krishna) Pranayama Breathing, or anything else based in Hinduism, Buddhism, Taoism etc., then most aspects of this prayer will be vital for you to go through. We suggest you read this through first, so you know what is involved, can think about what you are saying to God, and have your eyes open to your freedom.

Prayer of Repentance & Release from Personal or Hereditary Occultic involvements

Note: If you have practiced Yoga or Tai Ch'i exercises, Transcendental Meditation or Hindu, Taoist, Shinto, Buddhist or occultic meditations or chants, Pranayama breathing, any of the other Martial Arts, most Alternative Health Therapies; (all of which are based on Hinduism, Taoism, or other occultism) then aspects of the following prayer will apply to you and you will experience freedom as you pray.

Please don't just parrot the following prayer but think carefully about what you are saying to God. Please read it through first so you know what is involved. It is best to pray this aloud with a Christian witness or counselor present. We suggest a brief pause following each paragraph to allow the Holy Spirit to show any additional issues which may require attention.

"Father God, creator of heaven and earth, I come to you in the name of Jesus Christ your Son, and through His shed blood. I ask you for your protection as I pray the following prayer. I come as a sinner seeking forgiveness and cleansing from all sins committed against you, and others made in your image by myself or my ancestors. Please protect me and those whom I love. True Holy Creator God, in the name of the true Lord Jesus Christ, in accordance with Jude 8-10; Psalm 82:1 and 2 Chronicles 18, I request you to move aside all Celestial Beings, including Principalities, Powers and Rulers, and to forbid them to harass, intimidate or retaliate against me, and all participants in this ministry today. I also ask that You prevent these beings of whatever rank, to not be permitted to send any level of spiritual evil as retaliation against any of those here, or our families, our ministries or our possessions.

I believe in my heart that God the Father, raised His Son Jesus from death after Jesus had paid for my sins on the cross at Calvary, once for all.

Jesus Christ is therefore my Lord, my Savior, my Master and my Deliverer.

I choose to honor my earthly father and mother and all of my ancestors of flesh and blood, and of the spirit by adoption and godparents, but I utterly turn away from and renounce all their sins and iniquities. I forgive all my ancestors for the effects of their sins and iniquities on me and my children. I confess and renounce all of my own sins.

In the name of Jesus Christ of Nazareth, I turn from and renounce the denial by any of my ancestors, of the Gospel of Jesus Christ and of Jesus' work on the cross of Calvary.

I turn from and renounce Satan and all his works and every spiritual power or force of his, affecting me or my family, in Jesus' name.

I turn from and renounce the worship of all false Gods on the basis of Your Word recorded in Exodus 20 verse 3 which states **"Thou shalt have no other gods before me"** and I declare aloud that ***"Jesus Christ is my Lord."***

I turn from and renounce all occultic aspects and influences brought upon me by my ancestors' acknowledgement of Hindu, Taoist and other occultic Myths and Legends.

I turn from and renounce all divination and witchcraft as an abomination to God, in accordance with Deuteronomy 18:10-16.

I renounce all involvement in Idolatry by myself, my parents and all my ancestors.

I especially renounce the false gods and goddesses of Brahma, Shiva, Vishnu, Durga, Kali, Hunaman, Garnesha, and all the other idols.

I will destroy any objects in my possession that connect me with idolatry, witchcraft and the occult, including objects worn as jewellery for good luck or protection, and all objects of superstition, and I will not covet or keep or give away any precious metals from them.

I renounce the wearing of fetishes and their effects. I renounce all the superstitious fears that held me and my ancestors in idolatry and witchcraft, especially fear of Death, fear of spirits, fear of man and fear of trusting, in Jesus' name!

I renounce calling Brahma, Krishna, Buddha, or any other false god by the title of "Lord", as Jesus Christ alone is "King of Kings and Lord of Lords."

I renounce the Idolatrous practice of tattooing of the flesh specifically forbidden by God as the "cutting of the flesh", both as a practitioner and as the recipient, and the associated occultic demonic aspects.

I renounce the pride which would have led my ancestor into being tattooed or having their flesh cut or pierced.

I renounce the wearing of the "Kali dot" in the centre of the forehead, known as the "Third eye" or "Brow chakra" in occult groups, and I rebuke and reject every spirit of Divination or false spiritual insight which empowered it. I reject, break and renounce all agreement previously given by myself or my ancestors to be deceived by evil spirits.

I renounce all other witchcraft rituals and all curses spoken by me or my ancestors.

I renounce all talking to the dead and consulting with the dead which is described as the sin of "Necromancy" in Deuteronomy 18:11, and I renounce the kissing of dead loved ones and any evil spirit that has transferred to me from this practice.

I renounce all guidance by "familiar" or family spirits, especially the spirits posing as spirits of ancestors.

I renounce all songs involving the calling of spirits other than the Holy Spirit of God. I will listen to no other spirit than the Spirit of my Lord Jesus Christ.

I renounce the following of any "Guru" by me or my ancestors, whether as a "devotee" or out of curiosity.

I renounce the burning of Eastern incense because God says in Isaiah 66:3 "He that burns incense is as if he blessed an idol" or false god.

I renounce the false teachings of the "Vedas," the "Upanishads," and of Hindu or Buddhist priests or Gurus. I also renounce the teachings of Maharishi Mahesh Yogi, Satcha Sai Baba, and all other Gurus.

I renounce the taking of revenge on people and the associated guidance of demonic powers and their participation in such practices.

I renounce the entrapping of others and observing the helplessness of captives taken in revenge raids.

I renounce the practice of becoming a warrior and subsequent dedication to any war god idol, and all associated customs and practices.

I renounce the enjoyment of fighting, aggression and violence of all Martial Arts, of every kind and form.

I renounce all war dances and challenges which inspire fear in others.

I renounce the ritual murders or sacrifices of captives, and the fear of violent attack or assault and the fear of revenge.

I renounce the practice of human sacrifice to idols.

I renounce the practice of engraving or carving an image of false gods on talismans, bracelets or other items of superstition and lucky charms.

I renounce all customs associated with the non eating of certain food unless they had first been offered to idols, including "Vegetarianism".

I renounce all witchcraft/occult activity regarding the asking of those demonic powers to protect a war party and to bring it success.

I renounce the use of the fighting weapons and the associated occult practices and carvings engraved on these.

I renounce all fascination with snakes and serpents and the "seed of that old serpent", the devil.

I renounce all carved items worn & used as lucky charms.

I renounce all occultic dreams & demonic guidance given by evil spirits.

I renounce the belief in spirits dwelling under rivers, seas and harbours.

I renounce the chanted prayers to idols to make the crop(s) grow well, and the offering of foods to idols before eating.

I renounce every position held by an ancestor, whether Guru, teacher, or priest, who practised witchcraft.

I specifically renounce any love of position and power, avarice, or greed associated with the pride of these positions.

I renounce the calling of any man "Guru" or "Master", for Jesus Christ is my only Master and Lord.

I renounce all Yoga postures and beliefs, especially the "Serpent" posture, the “Cobra” posture, the “Lotus” posture, the “Elephant (Garnesha)” posture, and especially the mood swings and arguments it caused. I also renounce the Buddha posture, and the hip, knee and obesity problems it caused.

I also renounce the Hanuman "Three Little Monkeys" postures of Hear no evil; See no evil & Speak no evil and the spirits of divination associated with them, and the sexual problems it caused; and I will renounce all others by name as I remember them.

I renounce all “Pranayama” breathing exercises.

I renounce all confusion and depression, in the name of Jesus’ Christ!

I renounce all “False peace” associated with Hinduism, Taoism and their practices.

I renounce all fear of insanity, anguish, and death wish, suicide and death, in the name of Jesus Christ. He alone conquered death, and holds the keys of death and hell, and my life is in His hands now.

I renounce all emotional and sexual bondages related to these practices.

I renounce all anger, hidden anger, hatred, murderous thoughts, revenge and retaliation.

I renounce all unbelief, especially unbelief in the Holy Bible as God’s word, and compromise of God’s word.

I renounce treating God’s words as equal with, or of less value than the books of false religions.

I renounce those aspects of the Vedas, the Upanishads and other so-called Holy Books that are not acceptable to God.

I renounce all sickness and infirmity resulting from any of the above practices from which I have repented now.

I renounce and forsake all involvement in all forms of sorcery, divination, astrology, in the name of Jesus Christ.

I ask you Father God, to effectively nail to the cross of Jesus all records and laws written against me.

Holy Spirit, I ask that you show me anything else that I need to do or to pray in order to be free of the consequences of these sins.

(Pause, while listening to God, and pray as the Holy Spirit leads you.)

In the name of Jesus Christ I now rebuke all evil curses, breaking their power, and I loose myself and my children from them; all inherited or ancestral curses, curses from others; all evil words spoken by parents, teachers, old friends, relatives, spouses, all witchcraft or voodoo assignments, and all curses stemming from my culture. I now break the power of all charms, hexes, spells, psychic powers, bewitchments, witchcraft, sorcery, incantations, impartations, or assignments that have been put upon me or my family line from any person or group, living or dead, or from any occultic or psychic sources, including any familiar spirit assigned to me by Satan at my birth. I rebuke all connected and related spirits and command these to leave me now, in the mighty name of Jesus Christ.

I break every remaining soul tie that is ungodly with persons and groups in my past, in the name of Jesus Christ.

I renounce the ungodly soul tie with (cult group - mention name); with (mention person's name) who led me into the occultism of Martial Arts, Tai Ch'i, Transcendental Meditation, Yoga, Alternative Health Therapies, Astrology, Sorcery, Divination, (name practice); with the hypnotist (name); with (name) who led me into drugs; and with (name/s) that I had sinful sexual relations with (adultery, fornication, homosexuality, bestiality etc.) and also with any person whose blood was transfused or whose organ was transplanted into me.

I renounce all these and any other ungodly soul ties (mention other names that are appropriate) and I command the spirits of all these soul ties to leave me now in the name of Jesus Christ. I gather those ungodly soul ties together now and cut them through with the Sword of the Spirit of God. I now ask my Heavenly Father to reaffirm the Godly soul ties that I have with my spouse, children, and with members of the Body of Christ.

Now dear Father God, I ask humbly for the blood of Jesus Christ, your Son, to cleanse me from all these sins I have confessed and renounced, to cleanse my spirit, my soul, my mind, my emotions and every part of my body which has been affected by these sins, in Jesus' name!

I renounce every evil spirit associated with all these areas and all other sins, and I command in the name of Jesus Christ for every evil spirit to be bound and to leave me now, harmlessly on my natural breathing, touching or harming no-one, and go to the place appointed for you by the Lord Jesus Christ, never to return to me or my family. I call on the name of the Lord Jesus to be delivered of these spirits, in accordance with the many promises of the Bible.

I ask to be delivered of every spirit of sickness, infirmity, curse, affliction, addiction, disease or allergy associated with these sins I have confessed and renounced. I surrender to God's Holy Spirit and to no other spirit all the places in my life where these sins have been. I ask you, Lord, to fill me with your Holy Spirit now, according to the promises in your Word. I take to myself the whole armor of God in accordance with Ephesians Chapter Six, and rejoice in its protection as Jesus surrounds me and fills me with His Holy Spirit. I enthrone you, Lord Jesus, in my heart, for you are my Lord and my Saviour, the source of eternal life. Thank you, Father God, for your mercy, your forgiveness and your love, in the name of Jesus Christ, Amen."

If you have difficulty doing this, then please contact a competent Christian leader near you to assist you. Find Bible-believing Christians and spend time with them. Explain to them you are coming out of serious deception and need their encouragement and support at least until you are firmly on your feet and maturing in your relationship with the Lord Jesus Christ. If some disappoint you (probably through not understanding your need) don't be put off, there are caring Christians around who can and will help. If all else fails, please contact the publishers and we'll try and locate someone mature who can help you in your region. It is very important that you sever all of your ties with all occultic groups and practices.

Appendix - Reincarnation: Karma of Hopelessness

From the philosophical concept of Yin and Yang comes the belief in reincarnation. This belief is common to almost all Eastern religions, as well as Martial Arts. If a life ends, it must have a new beginning, it is claimed, because we exist in some form forever, until we reach nirvana, or heaven, or some type of eternal bliss where we achieve the goal of reaching immortality as gods. Although there are variations on this theme, virtually all Eastern religions claim this fundamental belief. There are two main streams of this belief. For Hinduism, this is achieved through much yoga. Buddhists believe that after death souls rejoin the "Universal Consciousness" or "World Soul," in much the same way as a drop of rain water falls into the ocean. George Lucas's "Star Wars" films portrayed this belief well. "The Force" is claimed to be available to the "initiated" who may use these mystical powers for good or evil. This is saying that God is an impersonal force and also the source of the concept of both good and evil.

Regarding reincarnation, or living over and over until we attain perfection, a friend pointed out that this would only make sense if the world population were constant, rather than growing at such a rapid rate over recent decades. On another occasion, a fourteen-year-old youth asked the vital and well-thought question: "If reincarnation were true, then what Karma did we have to work out during our first lifetime?" The answer is, "None, of course" because we hadn't lived before.

The following are notes from a video by a Christian who was an ex-Hindu Brahmin

The mystery of the Gospel challenges Hindus

"For me, who am less than the least of all saints, this grace was given, that I should preach among the Gentiles the unsearchable riches of Christ; And to make all see what is the fellowship of the mystery, which from the beginning of the ages has been hidden in God, who created all things through Jesus Christ; to the intent that now the manifold wisdom of God, might be made known by the church to the principalities and powers in the heavenly places, according to the eternal purpose which He accomplished in Christ Jesus our Lord." (Ephesians 3:8).

This mystery is explored in a Sanskrit Mantra Prayer

"The one who is born of the Spirit, I praise your name!

The one who is born of a virgin, I praise your name!

The tree on which love was sacrificed, I praise your name!

The person who has wounds on the body, I praise your name!

The one who walks on water, I praise your name!

The one who has victory over death, I praise your name!"

This One is the Mystery of God to Hindus. Christians know Him!

Hindus know that they have the sting of sin, just as a Moslem believes that the sin of Adam continues throughout his life.

Another Hindu prayer cries; "God release me (or save me) from all the bondage of sin!"

In the 10th book of Rig Veda #129 is this question; "Who is the God to whom we shall alone give our oblation? He is the Lord of the whole world. He who holds the earth and sustains everything!"

"Who is the God who is the giver of power?" The Lord of people!

In the Upanishads 1:3 "God can not be known by human mind unless He shows Himself by His grace." Hindu writings say that: "God will take a Human body and sacrifice it to take away sin." The Bagavada Gita (200 B.C.) says, "I am the way. He who worships me will not perish. I will deliver you from the bondage of sin. I am the beginning and the end. Come to me and I will give you peace and Eternity. There is only one God."

The Hindu temple is laid out exactly as was Moses' temple, including a stone outside and a bull (sacrifice) inside. It has a "Holy Place" and a "Most Holy place," and a curtain. The details are given in Rig Veda but no reasons are given there. The Bible gives the reasons as foretelling Christ.

Rig Veda says that the priest must eat the flesh of the sacrifice to be cleansed of sin. GURU means GU (sin) RU (destroyer) i.e. SIN DESTROYER (and "destroyer of darkness"). Jesus Christ is the only true SIN DESTROYER or true GURU!

The Hindus have taught individual reincarnation for millennia. The problem is that is wasn't in their original religious beliefs. Rig Veda 9:5 says “Those who worship idols and objects will end in utter darkness.”

In the Gita it asks; “Can anyone receive the (stem) of God by worshipping a stone?” Terms about the “Rebirth cycle” are not found in any of the ancient Sanskrit writings. The belief in reincarnation came into Hinduism after these books were written to justify unbelief in God’s judgement on sin. The Vedas and Upanishads were written before Hinduism and do not mention the word “Hinduism.” There were many religions before they merged under the one name of “Hinduism.”

Despite this, they believe that a person's soul moves from body to body in a birth-death-rebirth cycle. According to the Law of KARMA if you live a good life you will move into a higher life form, while a bad life is punished by going down the scale - so you could come back as a cow or dog or even an insect etc. This is a major reason why Hindus won’t eat meat - it might be a relative! Karma is a Hindu method of spiritual accounting.

This reasoning says that if you see a person suffering you shouldn’t help them as they are paying for sins committed in a previous lifetime. Abortion is perfectly acceptable to reincarnationists because they believe the aborted foetus is simply having his or her entry into personhood "rescheduled."

An illustration may help. According to the Law of Karma, a husband who beats his wife in this life must return in a subsequent life as a wife who is beaten by her husband. The person who commits a crime must become the victim of the same crime. This requires that someone else must commit this crime, who in the future must also become a victim, and so it goes on and on forever. You can see the Law of Karma actually perpetuates evil, and cannot overcome it. Consider the implications of this belief. If Karma is true, what evil must we face as future reincarnations of butchers such as Hitler, Stalin, Chairman Mao, Pol Pot, Idi Amin and others return to pay for their crimes in like manner!

Never-ending Cycle

Hindus speak of the "Wheel of Reincarnation." This means that each lifetime is spent working off the Karma of previous lives. Mahatma Gandhi called this "a burden too great to bear." Yoga was developed as a means of escaping this endless cycle of death and rebirth. It is claimed that if you reach high enough up this scale you will become God, or a god, or one with the universe, or enter the godhead. This belief is shared by Hindus, New Agers and other groups such as the Mormons and Theosophists.

According to Hindu tradition, at the beginning of the Path of Karma, the three Gunas or "Qualities of Godhead" were in perfect balance in the void - the nothingness from which everything comes and to which it all returns. Apparently something happened to cause an imbalance in this godhead, and the prakriti or manifestation began which brought about the illusion which we experience as the universe today. Confusing, isn't it!

What they are actually teaching is that bad karma actually began with an imbalance of their godhead itself, and so it is built into the very fabric of their universe. This means there is no escape - with or without Yoga - so Karma is a belief of hopelessness.

In more recent times this teaching has come to us in the west in a more subtle form through a number of people. Of particular note are actress Shirley MacLaine, astrologer Jeanne Dixon, mystic Edgar Cayce, songwriter Richard Bach in his hit 'Jonathon Livingston Seagull,' writers Ruth Montgomery and more recently Elisabeth Kubler-Ross. All these people reject the Bible's statements about judgement for sin by God. Aren't they in for a surprise!

These theories have an obvious appeal for many Westerners, for it gives the promise that life goes on and we get as many chances to get it right as we need. If reincarnation did actually happen then man has no compelling reason in this life to make peace with a righteous God, or even to treat his fellow man with any love or respect. Rabi Maharaj, the male members of who's family have been gurus for many generations, says that those supporting reincarnation in the West have got it all wrong - he said reincarnation is a punishment according to Hindu beliefs, not a benefit.

Do We Really Have Past Lives?

If reincarnation is true, why don't most of us have recollections of those past lives? Very few people even claim to. Those who do have been involved in some form of psychic or occultic activity. If we can't remember mistakes made and lessons learned then I wonder what is the point of living over and over again?

Some have argued that we have subconscious memories of these events which can be revealed through hypnotherapy and which benefit us at an unconscious level. If this were true then human beings both individually and collectively should be living better lives and there should be less evil in the world. Every news report proves that is not true.

There are even people who try to quote the Bible to support their belief in reincarnation. One of their main references is John 3:3, where Jesus told Nicodemus that to see the Kingdom of God one must first be born again. Jesus was not teaching that a series of rebirths were necessary to achieve perfection. Nicodemus expressed puzzlement and spoke of a second physical birth similar to reincarnation, but Jesus promptly corrected him. Jesus did not expound the Law of Karma, He refuted it. Jesus clearly spoke of a spiritual plane and not a physical one.

There are other Scriptures which clearly refute reincarnation. "It is appointed once for a man to die and after this comes the judgement." (Hebrews 9: 27) James, the brother of Jesus, wrote "You do not know what your life will be like tomorrow. You are just a vapour which appears for a little while, and then vanishes away." (James 4:14)

The Bible clearly teach that life in human form is a temporary state. Theories of our preexisting eternally are not supported by the Bible. Reincarnation is a poor and false substitute for the hope of resurrection which all believers in Jesus Christ have. Even if reincarnation were true, the Atonement by Jesus at Calvary makes unnecessary any repeated cycle of rebirth. Jesus also said **"For my Father's will is that everyone who looks to the Son and believes in Him will have eternal life, and I will raise him up at the last day."** (John 6:40)

The issue of sin - evil - was dealt with at Calvary. Jesus has already shown the way. Buddha, and all the other so-called gods and prophets are still in their graves, but Jesus rose from the dead!

For those who have accepted Jesus Christ as Lord and Savior, when we die we will go to be with Him. Those who haven't accepted Jesus go to a place of eternal torment. From the point of death onwards, spiritual changes are impossible.

Reincarnation is a false belief without hope. We will never become gods nor be equal with God. We will not merge with Him. God's promise is that we shall see Him face to face. The distinction between me - a creature - and God my creator will always remain.

References

1 "Practical Handbook on Kung Fu, Tae Kwondo, Tai Chi, Iaido & Shinto Ryu," by Fay Goodman, published by Hermes House, 1998, 2000, p 6
2 "A Christian Analysis of Tai Ch'i," by Andrew McIntosh
3 "Bob Larson Speaks out on Martial Arts," Bob Larson, Article, 1977.
4 "A Christian Analysis of Tai Ch'i," by Andrew McIntosh
5 "Why I Quit Karate," by Bill Rudge, p 5
6 "Out from Darkness," by Ben Alexander, pp 150-151.
7 "Larson's Book of Cults," Bob Larson, (Tyndale) 1982, p300 & 304
8 "Second Warning," by Barry Smith, 1985, p143
9 "Psychic Forces & Occult Shock," by Dr. John Weldon & Dr. Clifford Wilson (Global)
10 "A Christian Analysis of Tai Ch'i," by Andrew McIntosh
11 "Larson's Book of Cults," Bob Larson, Tyndale, 1982, p300
12 "Practical Handbook on Karate, Aikido, Ju Jitsu & Judo," by Fay Goodman, published by Hermes House, 1998, 2000, page 9
13 "Practical Handbook on Karate, Aikido, Ju Jitsu & Judo," by Fay Goodman, published by Hermes House, 1998, 2000, p 50
14 "Practical Handbook on Karate, Aikido, Ju Jitsu & Judo," by Fay Goodman, published by Hermes House, 1998, 2000, p 84
15 Professor Kano quoted in Kay Goodman, "Guide to Karate..."
16 "Practical Handbook on Kung Fu, Tae Kwondo, Tai Chi, Iaido & Shinto Ryu," by Fay Goodman, published by Hermes House, 1998, 2000 p12
17 ibid p101
18 ibid p 69
19 "A Christian Analysis of Tai Ch'i," by Andrew McIntosh
20 "A Christian Analysis of Tai Ch'i," by Andrew McIntosh
21 "The Holy Tradition," handbook, a 30-page booklet with the official version of the Puja in both Sandskrit and English, p 5.
22 Article by Brooks Alexander, Spiritual Counterfeits Project, PO Box 4308, Berkeley CA 94704, USA, 1989, p 3
23 "Understanding Alternative Medicine (Holistic Healing in the New Age)," by Roy Livesay, (New Wine Press).
24 video "Gods of the New Age," Jeremiah Films
25 "Yoga," article by Spiritual Counterfeits Project, 1990
26 "Raja Yoga," by Swami Vivikananda, Ramakrishna-Vivikananda Centre, New York, 1955, pps 22-23
27 "The Yoga of Light - Hatha Yoga Pradipika," by Yogi Swami Svatmarama, translated from Sandskrit by Hans-Ulrich Rieker. p 23.
28 "Yoga: The Method of Re-Integration" Alain Danielou, University Books New York, p. 17 & 18
29 "Teaching Asanas: an Ananda Marga Manual for Teachers. Amrit Publications, A'nanda Ma'rga 1973, pps 43,44
30 "The Deceptions of Martial Arts," Fred Grigg, (Mandate Ministries) p24
31 "The Deceptions of Martial Arts," Fred Grigg, (Mandate Ministries) p25

References from Article "A Christian Analysis of Tai Ch'i" by Andrew McIntosh:

"The Tao of Tai Chi Chuan" by Jou, Tsung Hwa.
"Tai Chi Chuan" by Chee Soo.
"The Spirit of Tai Chi Chuan, Movements of Magic," by Bob Klien.
"New Age Medicine (A Christian perspective on Holistic Health)," by Paul C Reisser M.D., Teri Reisser, and John Weldon, (Intervarsity Press).
"More Understanding Alternative Medicine (Holistic Healing in the New Age)," by Roy Livesay, (New Wine Press).
"Second Warning," by Barry Smith.
"Healing at Any Price," by Samuel Pfeifer, M.D., (Word Publishing).
"Schemes of Satan," by Mike Warnke, (Victory House, Inc.).
"In Search of New Jawbones," by Ray Comfort, (Living Water Publications).

"Christianity for Sceptics," by Dr. Steve Kumar, (Life Foundation, Auckland, NZ).
"Evidence that demands a verdict, Volume 1," by Josh McDowell, (Here's Life Publishers)
"Peace on Earth," Tract by Paul Simpson.
"Christian - have you been involved in the Martial Arts?" Tract by Paul Simpson
"The NIV Study Bible," 1985 by the Zondervan Corporation.
"Combating the New Age," Tape by Ex Hindu Indra Belsham, Radio Rhema Repeats

About Jubilee Resources International

God's commission for Jubilee Resources International is based on Ezekiel 33:1-9, and Luke 4:18-21. According to the Bible, Jubilee years were times of restitution. Debts were cancelled, slaves set free, families reunited and lost or forfeited inheritances restored. Every year was prophetic of the ministry of Jesus Christ. The Jubilee was proclaimed on the basis of the work of the High Priest on the Day of Atonement - so Jesus Christ's liberating ministry is founded on His atoning work. Jesus began His public ministry by reading the passage from the prophet Isaiah (Luke 4:18-21). All the liberties of the Jubilee year are now available to us through the redemptive work of Jesus Christ at Calvary, and we all have the responsibility to preach this Gospel of Redemption and Restoration to full Relationship with Yahweh/Father God. When Yeshua/Jesus Christ returns, God's people will be totally free from all sin, sickness and disease, death and curse. The Biblical Jubilee will then be fully realized.

Resources in print book, eBook, audio & video formats are available in English, with paper & eBooks in Spanish, German, French, Italian, Portuguese-Brazil, Polish, Russian, Dutch, Swedish, Danish, Finnish, Hungarian, Romanian, Slovak, Czech, Greek, Afrikaans & Tagalog, with other languages pending.

About the Author:

Selwyn R. Stevens,

Ph.D; D.Min.; M.I.S.D.M.; M.E.A.C.M.

is the President of Jubilee Resources International Inc. a New Zealand-based educational and religious organization involved in informing and equipping Christians of all denominations how to reach the lost and deceived in cults, the occult and secret societies such as Freemasonry. Author of over 35 books (and co-author of two), including twelve Best Sellers, an International Speaker (on five continents) and ordained minister. Dr. Stevens is a third-generation preacher, and has been involved in various Christian groups, and also maintains an active interest in national and world affairs and politics. Dr. Stevens is a Foundation Member of the International Society of Deliverance Ministers, founded by Dr. C. Peter Wagner and convened by Dr. William Sudduth of Virginia, USA; and Apostolic Overseer of the Alliance of African Christian Churches & Ministries based in Zambia. Regular Facebook and e-mail teaching and mentoring is also provided to many Christian leaders across Africa, Asia, Latin America & Caribbean resulting in tens of thousands being equipped for service to the Kingdom of God.

Additional Resources Available by

Selwyn R. Stevens

www.jubileeresources.org (Webshop)

Plus comprehensive range of free tracts to download

Dealing with Curses & Generational Iniquities. This teaching offers hope for all Christians that they can be released into the blessings of God and forever leave behind iniquities and curses that have kept them captive, perhaps their whole families for generations. This explains the twelve major curses that people may have operating in their families, and what to do about them. It also includes new material on the curses over Scottish, English, Irish, Welsh and Scandinavian people, plus many other national and ethnic groups. This teaching has been taught in several nations with much fruit for personal, family and community liberty. Best Seller
Book, E-book, MP4 & DVD

Dealing with Demons: *Insights into evil spiritual influences.* This popular teaching provides outstanding insights regarding evil spiritual influences that exist in the world in which we live today, and then goes further to show us what to do about it. Best Seller
Book, E-book, MP4 & DVD

Insights into Martial Arts, Tai Ch'i TM & Yoga. Much of the western world has seen an explosion of these practices. For many, their involvement has became close to a religion, adopting belief systems, mind sets and practises inconsistent with the teachings of the Bible. Best Seller
Book, E-book, MP4 & DVD

Treated or Tricked - Alternative Health Therapies Diagnosed. Many people are now trying Alternative Health Therapies. This book explains the various medical & spiritual healing methods; investigates whether the "Energy/Life Force" is scientific or spiritual; and describes almost 80 different Alternative Therapies, from Aromatherapy to Zone therapies. Also examines reasons why some are not healed & how to overcome these failures Biblically. Co-authored with Dr. Badu Bediako, (former Assoc. Professor of BioChemistry.) Best Seller
Book, E-book, MP4 & DVD

How to Recognize the Voice of God. How does God communicate to His people? How will you know when it is Him speaking to you? This very practical teaching has already helped many.
Book & DVD

Raising a Blessed Generation. The goals of this teaching are three-fold:

Goal 1: To understand what Blessing is and the Power it has for our lives today;

Goal 2: To Identify and Recover any missed blessings in my own life;
Goal 3: To Begin to Learn How to Bless others, especially our children & grandchildren! Identity and gender confusion is caused by the failure of parents & grandparents to speak identity and destiny into the young ones. Best Seller
Book, E-book, MP4 & DVD

Daniel and the Star Chasers. The counterfeit of Astrology has hidden what God wanted His people to know about the Gospel message in the stars. Daniel taught that truth to the Magi of Asia, and that nearly caused the War of the Continents half a millennium later. Only in recent decades has mankind had the technology to uncover what the Magi saw. Following Daniel's instructions, they went to see the King of Kings and submit their kingdoms and empires to His.
Book, E-book, MP4 & DVD

The Christian Life & the Role of the Fivefold Ministry. The Christian church is being increasingly side-lined in social debate. Have we ceased to be the Salt and Light commanded by Jesus Christ? The Solution: become real Christians! But what does that entail? Then, how are Christians to be governed? God provided the Fivefold ministry to do that. What does that look like? Best Seller
Book, E-book, MP4 & DVD

Help! The Sheep are Escaping: Understanding the Exodus From Church to God's Ecclesia. For most Christians in the West, "church" isn't working! The Old Wineskin cannot compete any longer, as God raises up His New Wineskin to fulfil His end-time purposes. The solution is for "church" to become Ecclesia and for participation with appropriate equipping, releasing and accountability.
Book, E-book, MP4 & DVD

Biblical Healing Training Manual. This thorough examination of Biblical physical healing is the result of many years of experience as well as training under some of the world's best Bible teachers. There are many "How To's", practical prayer and ministry guidelines, reasons why some aren't healed, and what we can do about them, etc. Hundreds have been healed, & many congregations have been empowered to commence regular Healing services with Christ-glorifying results. Best Seller
Book, E-book, MP4 & DVD

Fatal Faith - the Cult Counterfeit of Christianity. This book explains how cults develop and what patterns to avoid. Key Christian and Cult beliefs are compared with the main active cults. How to handle door-knockers, cult exiting, pre-cult spiritually-abusive churches; and how to protect young people from cults. Major ancient & modern heresies examined. Best Seller.
Book, E-book

The New Age - the Old Lie in a New Package. New Age & Bible beliefs and practices compared, including Reincarnation and Past lives, Astrology, the New Age pseudo Messiah, Self-worship & our Deity-potential. Energy/ Life Forces are examined, and the occult involvement of most holistic health gurus. Best Seller
Book, E-book

Discerning the Past to See the End Times: *Islam's Role in the Return of Jesus*. The statue in Nebuchadnezzar's dream, interpreted by Daniel, gives us a clear picture of the various empires that have sought domination of the Middle East and beyond. World events circle around this area of vital interest to God and His people. The Bible is a Middle Eastern book, not a European or American book. The context of the empires of the statue give us vital clues about the Empire of the Beast to come! Best Seller
Book, E-book, MP4 & DVD

Signs & Symbols: Cult, New Age & Occult Insignias & What They Mean. From Ananda Marga, Anarchy, & Ankhs, to Yin & Yang, Yoga & Zodiacs. By popular demand this book has a brief explanation & a Biblical comparison with dozens of insignias. 7th Edition, newly revised. Best Seller
Book, E-book

How to Minister to Change Lives and Communities. This comprehensive & practical training manual is for those who want to do effective ministry. This can include end-of-service and small-group ministry. Topics include Understanding the Spiritual Realm; Empowerment to Serve; Healing of the Body, & the Soul; Deeper Ministry by appointment & referral; & Biblical blessings to release identity and destiny. Best Seller
Book, E-book, MP4 & DVD

The Bible 101. A teaching manual introducing the Bible, explaining clearly it's purposes, origins, history, inspiration, symbolism, translations & versions, moving from milk to meat, study helps, rules of interpretation, and how to study it to get the best understanding.
Book, E-book, & MP4

Unmasking Freemasonry - Removing the Hoodwink. Written primarily for the wives & families of Masons to explain the curses brought on themselves and their families through the oaths; then learn how to deal with the effects. History & structure are explained simply. A Past Master who read this book immediately resigned from his Lodge. The prayer guidelines from this book are being used by many ministries worldwide. 7th edition with endorsement by C. Peter Wagner. Best Seller
Book, E-book, MP4 & DVD

Unmasking Mormonism - Who are the Latter-day Saints? Learn about LDS founder Joseph Smith on whose credentials this cult fails Bible tests, the Book of Mormon hoax, Mormon polytheism, true & false priesthood & authority. This book has caused many Mormons to cancel their baptisms & leave to seek the genuine Jesus Christ - the One from the Bible. Best Seller
Book, E-book, MP4 & DVD

Unmasking the Watchtower - Who are the Jehovah's Witnesses? This asks the questions many J.W.'s are being expelled for daring to ask! Check out the changeable prophecies and man-made doctrines of the Watchtower, the authoritarian leaders & their use of Mind-Control & manipulation of members, how to know the One True God, and how you can witness to and pray for a J.W. effectively. Best Seller
Book, E-book, MP4 & DVD

Rome's Anathemas: Insights into the Papal Pantheon. This vital book investigates Constantine's divorce of the Jewish roots of the Christian faith and its replacement with paganism; the Council of Trent rejected the Biblical basis of Luther's Reformation and cursed all who disagreed with them. In John, we read of the marriage feast at Cana. Realizing that the wine was gone and that she herself could not do anything, Mary tells Jesus, because He is the only One who could do something. Mary then gives the stewards her last recorded words and only command - one that we must consider for us to be saved. Mary said, *"Whatever He say to you, do it!"*
Book, E-book, MP4 & DVD

Additional Resources Available by

Selwyn R. Stevens

www.jubileeresources.org (Webshop)

Plus comprehensive range of free tracts to download

Made in the USA
Columbia, SC
14 September 2024

42336808R00046